Discover America
State by State

Teacher's Guide

Sleeping Bear Press

> ACKNOWLEDGMENT
>
> Our thanks to those teachers whose thoughtful comments and suggestions helped us develop this Teacher's Guide to the Sleeping Bear Press *Discover America State by State* classroom collection.

Copyright © 2006 by Sleeping Bear Press

All rights reserved. No part of this book may be reproduced in any manner without the express written consent of the publisher, except in the case of brief excerpts in critical reviews and articles.

Permission is hereby granted to purchasers of the *Discover America State by State* books to reproduce the Index for purposes of classroom use only.

All inquiries should be addressed to:

Sleeping Bear Press
310 North Main Street, Suite 300
Chelsea, MI 48118
http://www.gale.com/DiscoverAmerica

Sleeping Bear Press is an imprint of The Gale Group, Inc., a division of Thomson Learning, Inc.

Editorial, design, and production services provided by Publishers Resource Group, Austin, Texas.

Student activity sheets for each state title are available for download at:
http://www.gale.com/DiscoverAmerica

ISBN 1585362999

Printed in the United States of America

10 9 8 7 6 5 4 3 2

Discover America State by State Series

AK	L is for Last Frontier: An Alaska Alphabet	**ND**	P is for Peace Garden: A North Dakota Alphabet
AL	Y is for Yellowhammer: An Alabama Alphabet	**NE**	C is for Cornhusker: A Nebraska Alphabet
AR	N is for Natural State: An Arkansas Alphabet	**NH**	G is for Granite: A New Hampshire Alphabet
AZ	G is for Grand Canyon: An Arizona Alphabet	**NJ**	G is for Garden State: A New Jersey Alphabet
CA	G is for Golden: A California Alphabet	**NM**	E is for Enchantment: A New Mexico Alphabet
CO	C is for Centennial: A Colorado Alphabet	**NV**	S is for Silver: A Nevada Alphabet
CT	N is for Nutmeg: A Connecticut Alphabet	**NY**	E is for Empire: A New York State Alphabet
DC	N is for our Nation's Capital: A Washington, DC Alphabet	**OH**	B is for Buckeye: An Ohio Alphabet
DE	F is for First State: A Delaware Alphabet	**OK**	S is for Sooner: An Oklahoma Alphabet
FL	S is for Sunshine: A Florida Alphabet	**OR**	B is for Beaver: An Oregon Alphabet
GA	P is for Peach: A Georgia Alphabet	**PA**	K is for Keystone: A Pennsylvania Alphabet
HI	A is for Aloha: A Hawaii Alphabet	**RI**	R is for Rhode Island Red: A Rhode Island Alphabet
IA	H is for Hawkeye: An Iowa Alphabet	**SC**	P is for Palmetto: A South Carolina Alphabet
ID	P is for Potato: An Idaho Alphabet	**SD**	M is for Mount Rushmore: A South Dakota Alphabet
IL	L is for Lincoln: An Illinois Alphabet	**TN**	V is for Volunteer: A Tennessee Alphabet
IN	H is for Hoosier: An Indiana Alphabet	**TX**	L is for Lone Star: A Texas Alphabet
KS	S is for Sunflower: A Kansas Alphabet	**UT**	A is for Arches: A Utah Alphabet
KY	B is for Bluegrass: A Kentucky Alphabet	**VA**	O is for Old Dominion: A Virginia Alphabet
LA	P is for Pelican: A Louisiana Alphabet	**VT**	M is for Maple Syrup: A Vermont Alphabet
MA	M is for Mayflower: A Massachusetts Alphabet	**WA**	E is for Evergreen: A Washington Alphabet
MD	B is for Blue Crab: A Maryland Alphabet	**WI**	B is for Badger: A Wisconsin Alphabet
ME	L is for Lobster: A Maine Alphabet	**WV**	M is for Mountain State: A West Virginia Alphabet
MI	M is for Mitten: A Michigan Alphabet	**WY**	C is for Cowboy: A Wyoming Alphabet
MN	V is for Viking: A Minnesota Alphabet		
MO	S is for Show Me: A Missouri Alphabet		
MS	M is for Magnolia: A Mississippi Alphabet		
MT	B is for Big Sky Country: A Montana Alphabet		
NC	T is for Tar Heel: A North Carolina Alphabet		

Teacher's Guide Contents

Part 1 To the Teacher — vii
- Contents vii
- To the Teacher viii
- Lesson Structure x
- Sample Lesson Plans xi
- Correlation Charts xv

Part 2 Teaching Your State Book — xxv
- Contents xxv
- State Projects 1
- Before Reading 3
- During Reading 7
- After Reading 10

Part 3 Teaching Special Topic Lessons — 15
- Animals 16
- Arts and Entertainment 20
- Cities and Towns 24
- Culture and Heritage 28
- Ethnic Groups 32
- Geography and Climate 36
- Government 40
- Historical Events 44
- Historical Sites and Monuments 48
- Natural Attractions 52
- Natural Resources 56
- People in History 60
- Plant Life 64
- Sports and Outdoor Activities 68
- State Symbols 72
- Technology and Inventions 76
- Transportation 80

Part 4 Index — 85
- *Discover America State by State* Series 86
- Index 87

Discover America State by State Teacher's Guide

1. To the Teacher

To the Teacher . . . . **viii**
Welcome to *Discover America State by State* viii
Overview of the Teacher's Guide viii

Lesson Structure . . . . **x**
Teaching Your State Book: The Basic Lesson x
Teaching Special Topic Lessons x

Sample Lesson Plans . . . . **xi**
Plan A: Teaching Your State Book xii
Plan B: Teaching Your State Book
 and Special Topic(s) xiii
Plan C: Special Topic(s) as Supplement
 to Another Text xiv
Plan D: Four- to Six-Week Unit of Study xiv

Correlation Charts . . . . **xv**
National Council of Teachers of
English Standards xv
National Council for the Social Studies
Curriculum Standards for Early Grades xvii

Discover America State by State Teacher's Guide

To the Teacher

Welcome to *Discover America State by State*

The first Sleeping Bear Press state alphabet book was published in 1998. Since then, the *Discover America State by State* series has grown to include a book for every state and for the District of Columbia.

Perhaps you saw your first Sleeping Bear Press state alphabet book in a library, where the series traditionally has been available, or in your local bookstore. You might have realized the potential of these state alphabet books for many classroom uses, but you might never have managed to find time to follow through on the activities, projects, and other educational opportunities you knew these books could provide.

The Sleeping Bear Press *Discover America State by State* books are currently available in sets for classrooms, and their potential for classroom use is now supported by this Teacher's Guide, which has been informed by the thinking of teachers around the country. To make the best use of the lessons in the Teacher's Guide, it is suggested that each student have his or her own copy of your state alphabet book. In addition, it would be extremely beneficial to have a set of the 51-book *Discover America State by State* series in your classroom.

Overview of the Teacher's Guide

This Teacher's Guide has been organized to be as useful and as flexible as possible as you work your way through the alphabet book for your state, or when you use the entire *Discover America* series to compare states and important topics across states. It contains four sections: (1) To the Teacher, (2) Teaching Your State Book, (3) Teaching Special Topic Lessons, and (4) Index.

To the Teacher

- **Features** The section explains how this Teacher's Guide supports the teacher, meets student needs, and is easy to use. Also provided is a key to the icons used to differentiate instruction in the multilevel activities.

- **Lesson Structure** The intended use and lesson structure of the two types of lessons in this Teacher's Guide are presented, with a brief description of each category of activity and how students will use or benefit from the activities.

- **Sample Lesson Plans** Suggested pacing includes options for one week to up to six weeks of instruction. Sample lesson plans illustrate how you can pick and choose among the activities and projects to create lessons tailored to your objectives and your students. (See pages xi–xiv.)

- **Correlation Charts** The *Discover America* Teacher's Guide has been correlated to two sets of standards: the National Council of Teachers of English Standards and the National Council for the Social Studies Curriculum Standards for Early Grades. The correlation charts help you plan lessons to address specific standards. They may also guide you in supplementing other course materials with the *Discover America* state alphabet books to meet specific standards. (See pages xv–xxiv.)

- **Index** A complete index at the back of this Teacher's Guide helps you locate and compare information for your state or for all 50 states and the District of Columbia. You may wish to make the Index accessible to older learners to aid them in their *State to State* activities and research projects.

Features of the *Discover America Teacher's Guide*

Teacher Support for Teaching the Lessons

- Differentiated instruction: multilevel activities for learners of different ages and abilities, including English language learners and struggling readers
- A complete lesson for teaching your state book, including prereading, reading, and postreading activities, as well as student projects
- *Cross-Curricular Activities* and hands-on projects in social studies, geography, language arts, science, math, the creative and performing arts, and other fields
- *Special Topic Lessons* for in-depth treatment of topics such as *People in History*, *Cities and Towns*, *Technology and Inventions*, *Geography and Climate*, and many more
- *State to State* comparison activities using the *Discover America* 51-book series, placed in the Guide at point-of-use in the lessons
- Research projects to develop research skills at appropriate levels
- Opportunities for ongoing assessment of student progress

Teacher Information and Features

- Lesson planning suggestions and sample lesson plans
- Correlations to national content standards for social studies and English language arts
- Flexibility for choosing just what you need for your students and your time frame
- Easy-to-follow directions and teaching tips for tailoring instruction to three levels
- Attractive, readable design with ample side-panel space for your own notes
- Complete Index to locate and reference topics across states
- Downloadable student activity sheets at http://www.gale.com/DiscoverAmerica

Key to Multilevel Activity Icons

The activities and projects in this Teacher's Guide are designed for students at three levels and have been labeled accordingly. You will find that you have great flexibility to choose the best activities for your students. You will also find that you can involve all learners in the same activity or project by using the basic activity and then adding the more complex steps or questions to accommodate more advanced students.

*One-asterisk activities are easier and therefore appropriate for young children, for young English Language Learners (ELLs) and newcomers, and for struggling students.

**Two-asterisk activities are of average difficulty and are meant for a broad range of older elementary or more advanced younger students, and for transitioning or mainstreamed ELLs.

***Three-asterisk activities are challenging and often multistep. They are for above-average, advanced, or gifted students.

Lesson Structure

Teaching Your State Book: The Basic Lesson

Whether you simply want to introduce very young children to some aspects of your state's culture, or whether you use the book as a motivating supplement to your state history textbook, you will find the basic lesson helps you guide students through a meaningful sequence of knowledge-building activities that are also creative and fun. No matter how many times you use the lesson with your state alphabet book or other books in the series, each time will be a new experience, depending on the activities you choose to do and the students in your class. Following is the basic lesson structure.

- **State Projects (pages 1–2)** Suggestions for ongoing projects may be previewed so that you can assign them at the appropriate point in your state book lesson or unit.

- **Before Reading Activities (pages 3–6)** Multilevel suggestions include questions for developing background knowledge, followed by various types of prereading activities, including graphic organizers, previewing, and an introduction to genre as used in the books.

- **During Reading Activities (pages 7–9)** Multilevel reading suggestions include activities that promote reading fluency and comprehension, build vocabulary, and encourage students to connect the book to their own lives and use their creativity to express or interpret what they learn.

- **After Reading Activities (pages 10–13)** Multilevel suggestions include activities that follow up on prereading suggestions, as well as easy and more complex projects that provide synthesis and review of the entire book. These activities also provide opportunities for you to assess your students' progress.

Teaching Special Topic Lessons

Each beautifully illustrated *Discover America* state alphabet book is full of fascinating topics that can be developed on their own or in conjunction with your study of social studies or other areas. The *Special Topic Lessons* were developed in order to permit you to enrich your study of state history or to support meeting curriculum standards in other subjects with high-interest materials related to students' home state.

Seventeen topics, independent of each other and arranged alphabetically, begin with *Animals* and *Arts and Entertainment* and end with *Technology and Inventions* and *Transportation*. See page 15 for the list of the *Special Topic Lessons*.

Each four-page *Special Topic Lesson* follows the format below:

- **What Do Students Know?** Carefully chosen questions help introduce students to the topic and develop background knowledge. At least one question allows students to relate the topic to their own lives.

- **Cross-Curricular Activities** Multilevel activities from a variety of disciplines are meant to promote or help students demonstrate understanding. Projects are more complicated than activities and may have more steps, and they often lead to presentation of a student product.

- **Doing Research Projects** These projects help students develop research skills and carry out age-appropriate research assignments. Projects are leveled so that all students can participate in them. Some *State to State* activities may also involve research.

- **Thinking Critically** A series of questions challenge students to think, integrate new and old knowledge, and ponder the significance of what they have learned. Questions are leveled in a way that permits all learners to apply higher order thinking skills.

- **Extending Knowledge** These individual activities are designed to be carried on outside the class or even to extend beyond the end of the unit. We hope that they will be the extra incentive that feeds an interest or inspires a passion for something that caught a student's attention.

- **State to State** Appearing at the bottom of Special Topic pages, *State to State* helps you guide students to explore other states in the *Discover America* series and to compare and contrast them with your home state.

Sample Lesson Plans

You may choose to use the books in the *Discover America* series in any of several ways. For example, you might use your state's book to teach a one-week lesson or a longer unit about your state. Alternatively, you might use one or more of the state books to help teach a topic such as geography and climate, inventions, or famous people. Still another way to use the books is to reinforce a larger social studies, science, reading, or interdisciplinary unit you are teaching in your class. The charts below can help you select activities that are appropriate to your learning objectives, to your students' needs, and to your time frame.

Begin by deciding what learning objectives you wish to cover using the *Discover America* series and how much time you have to teach them. Here are some sample lesson plans that may help you determine how you will use these books in your classroom.

Plan A: Teaching Your State Book

The activities in this Teacher's Guide are organized into two parts. The first part, *Teaching Your State Book* (pages 1–13), contains state projects and multilevel activities that are designated *Before Reading, During Reading,* and *After Reading.* If you have only a few days or a week and you wish to teach your state book alone, selecting from these activities will suit your needs. If you have more time, you may spend two weeks by doing more activities and selecting a project.

Plan A: Teaching Your State Book

Lesson Plan Steps

Planning
Optional: Look at *State Projects* (pages 1–2) to begin making arrangements to implement a project.
  ↪ *e.g.* You may decide to arrange a field trip or to distribute folders for students to collect information.

Day 1
Introduce your state to students.
  ↪ *e.g.* Ask students the *Talking About Your State* questions on page 3.

Day 2
Select one or more *Before Reading* activities from pages 3–6, based on available time and your students' abilities and learning needs.
  ↪ *e.g.* *Help younger, ELL, or struggling readers work as a group to create a state topic cluster on the board (see page 4). Then preview the book with them (page 5).
  ↪ *e.g.* **/***Have older or more advanced students make a KWL chart. Then have them preview the book. (See page 5.)

Days 3–4
Select one or more *During Reading* activities from pages 7–9.
  ↪ *e.g.* *Guide students through echo reading (page 7). Then help them build their vocabulary by having them create personal dictionaries (page 8). Finally, allow students to explore their own artistic skills by doing the *Becoming an Artist* activity (page 8).
  ↪ *e.g.* **/***Have students read your state's book in pairs (page 7). Then help students connect the book to their own lives by guiding them in a group discussion, using the questions on page 8. Finally, encourage students to express themselves by acting out a scene in the book (page 9).

Day 5
Select one or more *After Reading* activities from pages 10–13.
  ↪ *e.g.* *Play the *Who/What Am I?* game on page 10.
  ↪ *e.g.* **/***Give students time to complete the KWL chart they began in the *Before Reading* activities. Then play the *Recalling the State Alphabet* game on page 10.

You may return to your Sleeping Bear Press state alphabet book several times during the year, rereading the book for different purposes and choosing different activities and projects. As the year progresses, you may incorporate higher-level activities or more involved research projects.

Plan B: Teaching Your State Book and Special Topic(s)

The second main section of this Teacher's Guide (pages 15–83) focuses on *Teaching Special Topic Lessons.* Plan B covers teaching your state alphabet book, plus a special topic. You may use this section to extend and deepen students' learning about their home state or to build cross-curricular units. This option will take two weeks or up to three or four weeks:

- About two weeks without many projects or *State to State* activities
- About three to four weeks with additional *State to State* activities and projects

To extend students' learning, go into more depth using your state book, and add other state books in the ***Discover America State by State*** series. Choose activities and projects from a *Special Topics* lesson (pages 15–83). If you want students to work on a project, introduce it at the beginning and encourage students to work on it throughout the unit.

Plan B: Teaching Your State Book and Special Topic(s)

Planning	Choose research projects and *State to State* activities you may wish to add. Decide which activities or projects to use for assessment.
Week 1	Use the Plan A one-week lesson plan through *During Reading*. Add additional activities, as desired. Postpone doing the *After Reading* activities.
Week 2	Add activities from Plan C, *Special Topics* such as those in the chart below.
Week 3-4	Finish up with the *After Reading* activities in Plan A, or select others from pages 10–13. Complete any longer term projects. Use these activities for Assessment.

Discover America State by State Teacher's Guide

Plan C: Special Topic(s) as Supplement to Another Text

You may wish to teach a *Special Topic* as part of Plan B (two to four weeks). Another option is to return to your state book or the *Discover America* series at a later time in order to teach a *Special Topic Lesson* to enhance a subject matter unit you are already teaching. For example, you might use your state alphabet book or the *Discover America* series to complement a science unit on geography and climate or on animals and their habitats. You will find rich support for reading instruction and for teaching English language arts lessons about rhyming words, poetry, and expository text. There are also many motivating writing and research activities to do as part of your English language arts curriculum. You and your students will find many uses for the state alphabet books in the *Discover America* series.

Any activity or project in this guide can be used in isolation or to enhance a larger unit of study. Pick and choose, based on your objectives, the time available, and your and your students' needs.

Plan C: Special Topic(s) as Supplement to Another Text

Suggested Time: 1–2 Weeks

- Assess prior knowledge about the special topic by asking questions from the section called *What Do Students Know?*
- Read to students or have students read the verse and (for older or more advanced students) the sidebar on the book page.
- Have students do an activity from two different subject areas in the *Cross-Curricular Activities* section (to pique interest).
- Have students do/get started on one project described in the *Doing Research Projects* section.
- To expand the lesson across states, use books in the Discover America series to have students complete at least on one *State to State* activity or project
- Use the critical thinking questions to lead students to think about the significance of what they learned by discussing one or more of the questions in the *Thinking Critically* section.
- Depending on time and students' interests and ability, do an *Extending Knowledge* activity.
- Return to *After Reading* activities.
- Presentation of final projects. Assessment: Select a project to use for assessment.

Plan D: Four- to Six-Week Unit of Study

Following and extending Plan B, you may create a four- to six-week unit of study by doing more activities in the basic lesson plan, choosing additional *Special Topic Lessons*, more *State to State* activities, and other projects.

Correlation Charts

National Council of Teachers of English Standards

National Council of Teachers of English Standards	Discover America State by State Teacher's Guide
1. Students read a wide range of print and nonprint texts to build an understanding of texts, of themselves, and of the cultures of the United States and the world; to acquire new information; to respond to the needs and demands of society and the workplace; and for personal fulfillment. Among these texts are fiction and nonfiction, classic and contemporary works.	8, 12, 22, 23, 28, 34–35, 47, 49–50, 61, 62, 63, 66, 70, 74, 75, 79, 83
2. Students read a wide range of literature from many periods in many genres to build an understanding of the many dimensions (e.g., philosophical, ethical, aesthetic) of human experience.	6, 7–8, 17, 28, 34–35, 45, 60–61
3. Students apply a wide range of strategies to comprehend, interpret, evaluate, and appreciate texts. They draw on their prior experience, their interactions with other readers and writers, their knowledge of word meaning and of other texts, their word identification strategies, and their understanding of textual features (e.g., sound-letter correspondence, sentence structure, context, graphics).	3, 4, 5, 6, 7, 8–9, 10, 17, 29
4. Students adjust their use of spoken, written, and visual language (e.g., conventions, style, vocabulary) to communicate effectively with a variety of audiences and for different purposes.	8–9, 11–12, 43, 60, 61, 62, 68
5. Students employ a wide range of strategies as they write and use different writing process elements appropriately to communicate with different audiences for a variety of purposes.	2, 10–11, 12, 20–21, 33, 52, 53, 54, 57, 60, 61–62, 65, 69, 77

National Council of Teachers of English Standards	*Discover America State by State Teacher's Guide*
6. Students apply knowledge of language structure, language conventions (e.g., spelling and punctuation), media techniques, figurative language, and genre to create, critique, and discuss print and nonprint texts.	20, 21, 56–57
7. Students conduct research on issues and interests by generating ideas and questions, and by posing problems. They gather, evaluate, and synthesize data from a variety of sources (e.g., print and nonprint texts, artifacts, people) to communicate their discoveries in ways that suit their purpose and audience.	2, 18, 22, 23, 25–26, 33–34, 35, 42, 46, 54–55, 58–59, 66, 70, 74, 78–79, 82
8. Students use a variety of technological and informational resources (e.g., libraries, databases, computer networks, video) to gather and synthesize information and to create and communicate knowledge.	2, 18, 22, 23, 25–26, 33–34, 35, 42, 46, 54–55, 58–59, 66, 70, 74, 78–79, 82
9. Students develop an understanding of and respect for diversity in language use, patterns, and dialects across cultures, ethnic groups, geographic regions, and social roles.	2, 18, 22, 23, 25–26, 33–34, 35, 42, 46, 54–55, 58–59, 66, 70, 74, 78–79, 82
11. Students participate as knowledgeable, reflective, creative, and critical members of a variety of literary communities.	18, 22, 25, 29–30, 33, 39, 41, 45, 49–50, 58, 63, 68, 69, 71, 75, 77, 79, 81, 83
12. Students use spoken, written, and visual language to accomplish their own purposes (e.g., for learning, enjoyment, persuasion, and the exchange of information).	2, 18, 22, 23, 25–26, 33–34, 35, 42, 46, 54–55, 58–59, 66, 70, 74, 78–79, 82

National Council for the Social Studies Curriculum Standards for Early Grades

National Council for the Social Studies Curriculum Standards for Early Grades	*Discover America State by State Teacher's Guide*
I. Culture	
Social studies programs should include experiences that provide for the study of culture and *cultural diversity,* so that the learner can:	
Performance Expectations	
a. explore and describe similarities and differences in the way groups, societies, and cultures address similar human needs and concerns;	20, 28, 30
b. give examples of how experiences may be interpreted differently by people from diverse cultural perspectives and frames of reference;	23, 29, 30, 31, 32, 46
c. describe ways in which language, stories, folktales, music, and artistic creations serve as expressions of culture and influence behavior of people living in a particular	20–21, 28, 29, 30, 31, 33, 67
d. compare ways in which people from different cultures think about and deal with their physical environment and social conditions;	29, 31
e. give examples and describe the importance of culture unity and diversity within and across groups.	29, 31
II. Time, Continuity, & Change	
Social studies programs should include experiences that provide for the study of *the ways human beings view themselves in and over time,* so that the learner can:	
Performance Expectations	
a. demonstrate an understanding that different people may describe the same event or situation in diverse ways, citing reasons for the difference in views;	47

National Council for the Social Studies Curriculum Standards for Early Grades	Discover America State by State Teacher's Guide
b. demonstrate an ability to use correctly vocabulary associated with time such as past, present, future, and long ago; read and construct simple timelines; identify examples of change; and recognize examples of cause and effect relationships;	26, 45, 46, 62
c. compare and contrast different stories or accounts about past events, people, places, or situations, identifying how they contribute to our understanding of the past;	28, 34, 46, 61
d. identify and use various sources for reconstructing the past, such as documents, letters, diaries, maps, textbooks, photos, and others;	7–8, 26, 27, 29, 41, 43, 44, 45, 49, 61–62, 63, 72
e. demonstrate an understanding that people in different times and places view the world differently;	45
f. use knowledge of facts and concepts drawn from history, along with elements of historical inquiry, to inform decision-making about and action-taking on public issues.	44, 45

III. People, Places, & Environments

Social studies programs should include experiences that provide for the study of *people, places, and environments,* so that the learner can:

Performance Expectations

a. construct and use mental maps of locales, regions, and the world that demonstrate understanding of relative location, direction, size, and shape;	25, 37
b. interpret, use, and distinguish various representations of the earth, such as maps, globes, and photographs;	3, 11, 25, 36, 37, 48, 51, 55, 59, 60, 69, 70, 77, 78, 81

National Council for the Social Studies Curriculum Standards for Early Grades	Discover America State by State Teacher's Guide
c. use appropriate resources, data sources, and geographic tools such as atlases, data bases, grid systems, charts, graphs, and maps to generate, manipulate, and interpret information;	3, 11, 36, 37, 39, 48, 59, 60
d. estimate distance and calculate scale;	22
e. locate and distinguish among varying landforms and geographic features, such as mountains, plateaus, islands, and oceans;	37, 38, 53, 55
f. describe and speculate about physical system changes, such as seasons, climate and weather, and the water cycle;	17, 36, 39, 66, 73
g. describe how people create places that reflect ideas, personality, culture, and wants and needs as they design homes, playgrounds, classrooms, and the like;	23, 26, 49, 51
h. examine the interaction of human beings and their physical environment, the use of land, building of cities, and ecosystem changes in selected locales and regions;	19, 26, 33, 56, 57, 58
i. explore ways that the earth's physical features have changed over time in the local region and beyond and how these changes may be connected to one another;	56, 57, 59
j. observe and speculate about social and economic effects of environmental changes and crises resulting from phenomena such as floods, storms, and drought;	38
k. consider existing uses and propose and evaluate alternative uses of resources and land in home, school, community, the region, and beyond.	57, 58, 59

National Council for the Social Studies Curriculum Standards for Early Grades	Discover America State by State Teacher's Guide
IV. Individual Development & Identity	
Social studies programs should include experiences that provide for the study of *individual development and identity,* so that the learner can:	
Performance Expectations	
b. describe personal connections to place–especially place as associated with immediate surroundings;	28, 29, 30
c. describe the unique features of one's nuclear and extended families;	29, 30
e. identify and describe ways family, groups, and community influence the individual's daily life and personal choices;	28, 29, 30
f. explore factors that contribute to one's personal identity such as interests, capabilities, and perceptions;	28, 29, 30
g. analyze a particular event to identify reasons individuals might respond to it in different ways;	46
h. work independently and cooperatively to accomplish goals.	9, 11, 13, 17, 18, 21, 22, 23, 24, 25, 26, 27, 28, 29, 30, 31, 32, 33, 34, 35, 37, 38, 39, 40, 41, 42, 43, 44, 45, 46, 47, 48, 49, 50, 51, 53, 54, 55, 56, 57, 58, 59, 60, 61, 62, 63, 64, 65, 66, 67, 68, 69, 70, 72, 73, 74, 75, 76, 78, 80, 81, 82, 83
V. Individuals, Groups, & Institutions	
Social studies programs should include experiences that provide for the study of *individual, groups, and institutions,* so that the learner can:	
Performance Expectations	
b. give examples of and explain group and institutional influences such as religious beliefs, laws, and peer pressure, on people, events, and elements of culture;	30

© Sleeping Bear Press. All rights reserved.

National Council for the Social Studies Curriculum Standards for Early Grades	Discover America State by State Teacher's Guide
e. identify and describe examples of tension between an individual's beliefs and government policies and laws;	42

VI. Power, Authority, & Governance

Social studies programs should include experiences that provide for the study of *how people create and change structures of powers, authority, and governance,* so that the learner can:

Performance Expectations

a. examine the rights and responsibilities of the individual in relation to his or her social group, such as family, peer group, and school class;	53, 54
b. explain the purpose of government;	40–41
c. give examples of how government does or does not provide for needs and wants of people, establish order and security, and manage conflict;	24, 40, 41, 42, 43
e. distinguish among local, state, and national government and identify representative leaders at these levels such as mayor, governor, and president;	40, 41, 42, 43
f. identify and describe factors that contribute to cooperation and cause disputes within and among groups and nations;	30
g. explore the role of technology in communications, transportation, information-processing, weapons development, or other areas as it contributes to or helps to resolve conflicts;	24–25
h. recognize and give examples of the tensions between the wants and needs of individuals and groups, and concepts such as fairness, equity, and justice.	46

National Council for the Social Studies Curriculum Standards for Early Grades	Discover America State by State Teacher's Guide
VII. Production, Distribution, & Consumption	
Social studies programs should include experiences that provide for the study of *how people organize for the production, distribution, and consumption of goods and services,* so that the learner can:	
Performance Expectations	
a. give examples that show how scarcity and choice govern our economic decisions;	57, 58, 59
c. identify examples of private and public goods and services;	24–25
d. give examples of the various institutions that make up economic systems such as families, workers, banks, labor unions, government agencies, small businesses, and large corporations;	24, 25
e. describe how we depend upon workers with specialized jobs and the ways in which they contribute to the production and exchange of goods and services;	25, 26, 27
g. explain and demonstrate the role of money in everyday life;	34
h. describe the relationship of price to supply and demand;	59
i. use economic concepts such as supply, demand, and price to help explain events in the community and nation.	59
VIII. Science, Technology, & Science	
Social studies programs should include experiences that provide for the study of *relationships among science, technology, and society,* so that the learner can:	
Performance Expectations	
a. identify and describe examples in which science and technology have changed the lives of people, such as in homemaking, childcare, work, transportation, and communications;	24, 25, 76, 77, 78, 80, 81, 82, 83

National Council for the Social Studies Curriculum Standards for Early Grades	Discover America State by State Teacher's Guide
b. identify and describe examples in which science and technology have led to changes in the physical environment, such as the building of dams and levees, offshore oil drilling, medicine from rain forests, and loss of rain forests due to extraction of resources or alternative uses;	57, 79, 82
c. describe instances in which changes in values, beliefs, and attitudes have resulted from new scientific and technological knowledge, such as conservation of resources and awareness of chemicals harmful to life and the environment;	82–83
d. identify examples of laws and policies that govern scientific and technological applications, such as the Endangered Species Act and environmental protection policies.	19
IX. Global Connections	
Social studies programs should include experiences that provide for the study of *global connections and interdependences,* so that the learner can:	
Performance Expectations	
a. explore ways that language, art, music, belief systems, and other cultural elements may facilitate global understanding or lead to misunderstanding.	28, 29, 30, 31
X. Civic Ideals & Practices	
Social studies programs should include experiences that provide for the study of *the ideals, principles, and practices of citizenship in a democratic republic,* so that the learner can:	
Performance Expectations	
a. identify key ideals of the United States' democratic republican form of government, such as individual human dignity, liberty, justice, equality, and the rule of law, and discuss their application in specific situations;	40, 41, 42, 43

National Council for the Social Studies Curriculum Standards for Early Grades	Discover America State by State Teacher's Guide
b. identify examples of rights and responsibilities of citizens;	41
e. explain actions citizens can take to influence public policy decisions;	43
h. examine how public policies and citizen behaviors may or may not reflect the stated ideals of a democratic republican form of government.	41, 42, 43

2. Teaching Your State Book

State Projects 1
*A selection of student projects to assign
for completion during study of your state*

Before Reading 3
Developing Background Information. 3
Making a Graphic Organizer 4
Previewing the Book 5
Talking about Genre: Verse and Prose 6

During Reading 7
Developing Reading Fluency 7
Learning History Through Illustrations 7
Connecting the Book to Students' Lives 8
Building Vocabulary 8
Bringing the Book to Life 9

After Reading 10
Bringing It All Together 10
Writing Prose and Verse 10
Postreading Projects 11
Connecting the Book to Students' Lives 12
Performing the ABCs 13

State Projects

Here are a number of student projects designed to be completed during the study of your state. You may wish to preview them in order to make assignments at the appropriate time.

Taking a Field Trip

If your city or town has a city or state museum, or a historical society or related organization, plan a field trip or arrange to have someone visit your class. If you live in a state capital, visit the capitol building. You could also choose to visit your town hall or some municipal department. Once you have arrived, collect or have students collect brochures and materials. If possible, take photos of students individually and in groups at the location. Back in the classroom, have students discuss what they learned on the field trip and create a display to which they can add throughout the unit.

Creating a Portfolio

Have each student keep a folder in which to put materials related to your state's history. Encourage students to collect pictures and information from newspapers and magazines, places they visit, the Internet, and so on. They could also keep their map, if they made one, and other activity materials in this folder. Pictures and information can be collected and used for collages, scrapbooks, and other projects. (See below.)

Making an Alphabet Quilt

Invite each student to choose a letter or a topic related to your state or your city (either repeating the alphabet item in the book or choosing a new one). Older and more advanced students might want to think of other things that represent the state or choose something from the sidebar information. Invite students to draw and label a picture of their item and thus add one "square" to an alphabet quilt. Have volunteers fill in any missing letters. Attach (pin, tack up, staple, glue) each sheet (running alphabetically left to right) in rows of five or six to some kind of backing (sheet, bulletin board, large sheets of cardboard) to make the quilt.

Levels of Difficulty

*Easiest, for younger or struggling students and for young English Language Learners (ELLs) and newcomers

**Average difficulty, for older on-grade-level students or more-advanced younger students and for transitioning or mainstreamed English Language Learners (ELLs)

***Most challenging, for above-average, advanced, and gifted students

Discover America State by State Teacher's Guide

Creating a State Scrapbook

Have students create a state scrapbook, using pictures and information that they collect in their portfolios as well as materials you provide, and photos from home and their field trip.

*Younger or less advanced students might make a class alphabet scrapbook, labeling the alphabet and pictures they use.

/*Older students might create an individual scrapbook, annotating each item with a few sentences or a descriptive paragraph.

Doing Research

Looking It Up *Have students choose one state feature they would like to learn more about. Younger, ELL, or struggling students might choose a famous person, a state attraction, or the capital city. Provide appropriate age-level reference materials: encyclopedias, nonfiction books, magazines, and so on. Then have the class gather information in the form of an illustrated booklet. Students could develop a topic sentence and outline before preparing the booklet.

Going Online **/***Older or more advanced students might take similar or more advanced topics, such as events, concepts, or political issues, and do their research using online resources. Students could work on developing an outline and topic sentences before presenting their findings in the form of a multimedia report, including images, quotations, and so on.

Creating a Rhyming Alphabet Book

Have students create a new illustrated rhyming alphabet book. They might produce a book for your city, a new one for the state, or one for the United States as a whole.

*You could work with younger, ELL, or struggling students to create a class or a group book, with everyone brainstorming and discussing ideas and then each student contributing an alphabet page to the book.

**Older or more advanced students might enjoy creating their own book with a four-line rhyme for each alphabet letter.

***You might want to encourage advanced students to do research and write sidebar text as well.

Levels of Difficulty

*Easiest, for younger or struggling students and for young English Language Learners (ELLs) and newcomers

**Average difficulty, for older on-grade-level students or more-advanced younger students and for transitioning or mainstreamed English Language Learners (ELLs)

***Most challenging, for above-average, advanced, and gifted students

Before Reading

Developing Background Information

Choose one or more of the following activities to access students' prior knowledge.

Talking About Your State You may want to introduce the state alphabet book by asking students some of the following questions:

- Have you taken any trips with your family or your class to see something special in [state name]? What did you see? Tell about it.
- Which places in [state name] would you like to see? Which would you tell a visitor to see? Why is each place special?
- Do you know the state [animal/bird/flag/flower/motto/song/tree]?
- What else do you think is special about our state?

Using a Map Help students locate your state on a map of the United States. Then provide each student with an outline map of the state.

*****Have younger, ELL, or struggling students trace the shape of the map with a finger. Then ask them to use their imagination to brainstorm suggestions about what the shape of the state resembles. (Does it look like a star? a square? a particular animal? What does it look like sideways or upside-down?) Invite students to color the map or use craft supplies to transform it into an object or animal.

/*Have more advanced or older students fill in the map, based on what they already know. They might put in the state capital, your city or town, other cities or towns familiar to them, landmarks, geographical features (for example, mountains and bodies of water), and so on. Collect or have students save this map in their portfolios to compare with a map they will make after working with the book. (See After Reading.)

Levels of Difficulty

*****Easiest, for younger or struggling students and for young English Language Learners (ELLs) and newcomers

**Average difficulty, for older on-grade-level students or more-advanced younger students and for transitioning or mainstreamed English Language Learners (ELLs)

***Most challenging, for above-average, advanced, and gifted students

Discover America State by State Teacher's Guide

Making a Graphic Organizer

Choose one of the following activities to organize what students know and will learn about the state.

Creating a Web or Cluster *For younger, ELL, or struggling students, begin a web by writing your state's name in a circle on the chalkboard. Ask students what they could tell someone about your state. Help them come up with topics such as *cities and towns, special places to visit, or things to do in the state*. Choose two or three topics, write each one in a circle, and connect each circle to the state name. Then have students brainstorm responses to the topics as you continue to connect the responses in a web.

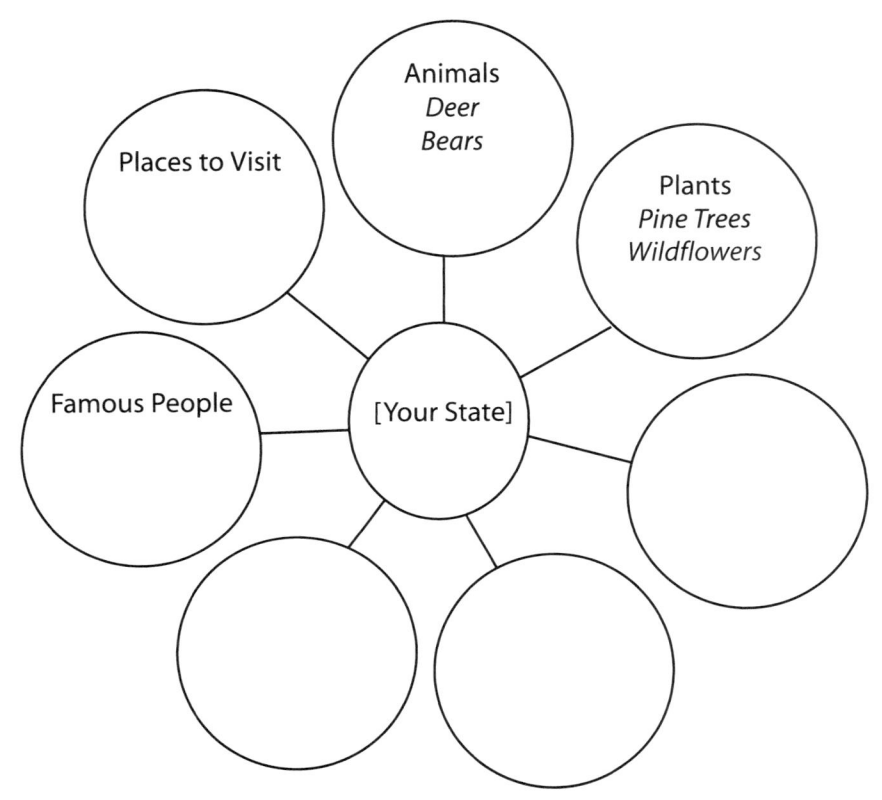

[Diagram: A central circle labeled "[Your State]" connected by spokes to surrounding circles labeled "Animals / Deer / Bears", "Plants / Pine Trees / Wildflowers", "Places to Visit", "Famous People", and three blank circles.]

**For more advanced or older students, have students brainstorm a list of topics connected with the state. You might start them off with a topic, such as animals or plants, and encourage them to generate more challenging topics, such as important people, geographic features, or famous buildings. Write each topic in a circle, and connect each circle with a radiating spoke to the state name. Have students brainstorm responses to each topic, either as a class or in small groups.

***You might want to have advanced students choose one category to create a web individually. Then have them share or combine their work in groups or as a class.

Levels of Difficulty

*Easiest, for younger or struggling students and for young English Language Learners (ELLs) and newcomers

**Average difficulty, for older on-grade-level students or more-advanced younger students and for transitioning or mainstreamed English Language Learners (ELLs)

***Most challenging, for above-average, advanced, and gifted students

Before Reading

Making a KWL Chart Invite students to create a KWL chart on poster paper. Fill in their answers for the first two columns, K and W: What do you **know** about the state? What do you **want** to know? Tell students that they will complete the third column, What did you **learn**? after they have finished the book. Be sure to save the chart. (See *After Reading.*)

K	W	L

Previewing the Book

Choose one or more of these suggestions to help students become familiar with the state book.

Getting an Overview *For younger, ELL, or struggling students, display the book cover and ask them to predict what the book is about. Then direct students' attention to the page(s) for the first letter of the alphabet. Ask how the letter A is illustrated or what part of the page represents the letter A. Then ask students about other objects in the illustration, and have them discuss their relevance. Guide students in discussing the entire context or scene in which the alphabet item appears. You might want to repeat this for letters B and C.

**For advanced or older students, have students flip through the book and ask them to describe how the book is organized (an alphabet book; organized by alphabetic objects that tell something about the state; every object is described in a brief verse as well as in a prose side column, or sidebar; and so on).

Browsing for Specific Information * For younger, ELL, or struggling students, display the book (or have students browse through it) page by page, looking for specific items. You might ask how many animals they can find in the book, whether they can find some famous people they recognize, or whether they can pick out some state symbols (animal, bird, flag, and so on).

Levels of Difficulty

*Easiest, for younger or struggling students and for young English Language Learners (ELLs) and newcomers

**Average difficulty, for older on-grade-level students or more-advanced younger students and for transitioning or mainstreamed English Language Learners (ELLs)

***Most challenging, for above-average, advanced, and gifted students

Discover America State by State Teacher's Guide

Talking About Genre: Verse and Prose

*For younger, ELL, or struggling students, select a verse, and read it to students. Ask whether the language is like the language they use every day. How is it different? You might elicit and discuss terms such as *rhyme, rhyming words, beat, rhythm*. Discuss which words rhyme, and help students hear the stresses or beats in each line.

**For more advanced or older students, have students flip through the book to choose a verse they like. Have volunteers read verses aloud. Ask students what they notice about the language, and elicit terms such as *poetry, verse, rhyme, rhythm*. Discuss which words rhyme, and help students hear the stresses or beats in each line. Ask students about the arrangement of the lines (position on the page, whether each line ends a sentence, and so on).

***If students examine several alphabet verses, ask whether the rhythm and rhyme patterns are the same or different. (Depending on your state book, the second and fourth lines may always rhyme, students might find words that don't quite rhyme, the rhythm of each verse may not be regular, and so on.)

**Have students find a page they like or use the verse page they chose. Read the sidebar (expository text) to students, or have a volunteer read it aloud. Ask students what they notice about the language and the content. Elicit terms such as *prose, information, nonfiction, facts, history*. Discuss the style and the tone, and ask students what the purpose of the book is (gives readers information, provides an enjoyable reading experience through humor and beautiful illustrations, and so on).

Note: *At this time you might want to introduce projects for students to work on as they proceed through the book. See* State Projects *on pages 1–2.*

Levels of Difficulty

*Easiest, for younger or struggling students and for young English Language Learners (ELLs) and newcomers

**Average difficulty, for older on-grade-level students or more-advanced younger students and for transitioning or mainstreamed English Language Learners (ELLs)

***Most challenging, for above-average, advanced, and gifted students

Before Reading

During Reading

Developing Reading Fluency

Echo Reading *For younger, ELL, or struggling students, read the first line of the verse, and have students echo you. After they have repeated each of the four lines, read the first two lines and then the last two, and finally help them echo the whole verse. You might want to continue this activity by pairing up students with adults such as parents, classroom aides, or volunteers. Students echo the adult's reading of selected pages.

Supported Reading **For students capable of reading the alphabet rhyme, encourage them to read the rhyme, with help as needed, to the adult. The adult will then read the sidebar text to the student, or help the student read it aloud, and discuss the content to ensure comprehension.

Peer Reading ***As a more challenging activity, have students work in pairs. Alternating page by page, one student reads the alphabet rhyme and the other reads the sidebar text. As they finish each page, have pairs create several questions as a comprehension check. The questions may then be used for a class or partner history trivia game.

Learning History Through Illustrations

Learning from Pictures *For younger, ELL, or struggling students, ask students to look at each picture. Which objects start with the featured alphabet letter? Which don't? What letters do those objects begin with? **Encourage older or more advanced students to discuss details in the illustrations and also to discuss the artistic medium and style of the illustrations. (Some artwork is done in watercolors, some drawn with chalk, and so on. In some books, leaves on trees are rendered through impressionistic dabs of color rather than through realistic drawings of leaves. Some drawings are almost as realistic as photos.)

/*Challenge students to use their powers of observation to extract or infer other information about the geography, climate, people, time period, and so forth.

Levels of Difficulty

*Easiest, for younger or struggling students and for young English Language Learners (ELLs) and newcomers

**Average difficulty, for older on-grade-level students or more-advanced younger students and for transitioning or mainstreamed English Language Learners (ELLs)

***Most challenging, for above-average, advanced, and gifted students

Discover America State by State Teacher's Guide

Becoming an Artist *Younger, ELL, or struggling students can do any number of art activities based on what they see on the page. They could, for example, trace, draw, or paint the state animal, bird, tree, or flower; make the state flag out of construction paper or other medium; use clay to sculpt boats, buildings, or bridges; cut out state pictures and make small collages; and so on.

**Older or more advanced students could learn more about some of the alphabet topics—for example, the state flag—and annotate their drawings with such information as when the flag was created, who designed it, who actually made it. If, for example, there were many versions of the state flag, students could draw and annotate the different versions.

Connecting the Book to Students' Lives

*For younger, ELL, or struggling students, ask questions that encourage students to connect their own experiences to what they are reading about in the book. For example, have you ever seen this animal? Have you ever visited this place? Have you ever eaten this food? Did you ever hear of this person? Invite students to talk about their experiences.

/*For older or more advanced students, encourage students to explore the significance of what they are reading. Why is/was this important? How did this change people's lives? What influence does/did this have on your own life? Would you like to do the kind of work that this person did? Why or why not?

Building Vocabulary

Creating a Personal Dictionary *For younger, ELL, or struggling students, have students create cards or a loose-leaf book, each card or page labeled with one alphabet letter. As they discover words to learn in the state alphabet book, have them copy the word and draw a symbol or picture to depict the definition. Encourage them to either dictate or write a brief definition or to use the word in a sentence.

/*Older or more advanced students may set up their dictionaries on the computer, printing out and illustrating pages or adding clip art and digital images. You may wish to review dictionary format with the class.

Making and Using Learning Cards *Have younger, ELL, or struggling students make a set of cards to help them learn any unusual vocabulary they find on the pages. Ask them to write the word on one card and to draw a picture that defines the word on a second card. As students accumulate cards, they can play a matching game in which they take turns turning over two cards at a time, remembering locations, and eventually turning over (and taking) matched cards.

Levels of Difficulty

*Easiest, for younger or struggling students and for young English Language Learners (ELLs) and newcomers

**Average difficulty, for older on-grade-level students or more-advanced younger students and for transitioning or mainstreamed English Language Learners (ELLs)

***Most challenging, for above-average, advanced, and gifted students

/*For older or more advanced students, the matching cards could consist of more complex vocabulary, including definitions of abstract ideas, and concepts. They could also include questions and answers about specific state features. Remind students to keep their cards for playing other games and for review.

Bringing the Book to Life

Reading or Memorizing Rhymes As students progress through the book, invite volunteers to read aloud their favorite rhyme(s). As they become more comfortable, encourage them to memorize and then recite their favorite rhymes, perhaps first to a buddy, then to a small group, and finally to the class.

Acting Out the Page *Encourage students to act out what they see on a page. They could act out animals, elements of the landscape, and people as well as events. Encourage them to use their imaginations.

Making Up Tunes and Dances *Invite small groups of students to make up songs or chants for the alphabet rhymes and present them. Later you might want to encourage students to make up movements or dances for the tunes. Animals and people may be obvious choices for dances, but students might also enjoy coming up with creative movements for inanimate objects as well as for concepts and feelings.

Acting Out Scenes **/***Older or more advanced students might enjoy acting out scenes from the book. They might reenact specific events, deliver lines from famous speeches, or do dramatic improvisations. They might also put on a class or a group play or create a PowerPoint presentation and narration in which each student reads (or recites from memory) one rhyme. More advanced pairs of students could recite the memorized rhyme, followed by a partner who reads the sidebar text and then recites the rhyme, so that students are alternating parts.

Levels of Difficulty

*Easiest, for younger or struggling students and for young English Language Learners (ELLs) and newcomers

**Average difficulty, for older on-grade-level students or more-advanced younger students and for transitioning or mainstreamed English Language Learners (ELLs)

***Most challenging, for above-average, advanced, and gifted students

After Reading

Bringing It All Together

Choose from among the following activities to help students integrate and summarize what they have learned. These activities may be used to assess students' understanding of their state.

Completing the KWL Chart Revisit the KWL chart that students created before reading. Invite them to complete the third column of the chart with what they learned about the questions they wanted to answer, as well as with other information they learned about their state.

Playing Who/What Am I? Have students play a riddle or guessing game in which someone gives a clue about a state object or feature and provides the first letter of the answer. *(I am the capital of Texas. My name starts with the letter A. What am I?)* The person who answers correctly might ask the next question, or you might prefer to call on volunteers.

*Younger, ELL, and struggling students might do this activity by looking at the pages as they formulate their questions.

/*Older or more advanced students might try asking questions from memory. Instead of providing the first letter, they may ask, *What letter does my name start with?* before the response can be given. Including information from the sidebar would step up the difficulty level considerably.

Recalling the State Alphabet Invite students to play a game in which they try to remember what item was featured for each letter of the alphabet.

*For younger, ELL, and struggling students, you might want to go consecutively from A to Z, give clues, and allow students to use the book as necessary.

/*For older or more advanced students, you might mix up the letters and include content from the expository text in the sidebar.

Writing Prose and Verse

Creating Verses Challenge students to make up their own state alphabet verses.

*For younger, ELL, or struggling students, preselect a four-line alphabet verse, and invite students to make up a new one about the same featured item. You might want students to work as a group and/or to reuse the first line of the book alphabet rhyme.

/*Older or more advanced students might work in pairs or individually to choose an alphabet letter and create a four-line alphabet rhyming verse about a state-related item not treated in the book.

Levels of Difficulty

*Easiest, for younger or struggling students and for young English Language Learners (ELLs) and newcomers

**Average difficulty, for older on-grade-level students or more-advanced younger students and for transitioning or mainstreamed English Language Learners (ELLs)

***Most challenging, for above-average, advanced, and gifted students

Writing Expository Text Encourage students to write about something new they learned about the state. Review how to organize and write expository text. Encourage use of the computer for those who are computer literate.

*Younger, ESL, or struggling students could write (or copy or dictate) and illustrate a sentence or two.

/*Older or more advanced students might write an expository paragraph or paper, illustrating it with photos, drawings, or other graphic material.

Postreading Projects

Making a Map Whether or not you worked with maps as a prereading activity, provide each student with a new outline map of your state. You may wish to use this activity as an assessment tool.

*Have younger, ELL, or struggling students cut out the map and paste it onto cardboard. Encourage them to fill in the map with any cities or famous places they learned about. When they are finished, ask them to pencil in lines that divide the map into six to ten jigsaw puzzle pieces. Invite them to cut up the puzzle pieces, exchange pieces with a partner, and put together each other's state map puzzle.

/*Have more advanced or older students fill in the map, this time creating a legend with icons for features such as forests or deserts, animals, industries, agricultural crops, buildings and monuments, and so on. When they are finished, invite them to compare this map with the map they made as a prereading activity.

Creating a Collage Have students use pictures and other materials they have collected in their portfolios and/or provide them with materials you have gathered (perhaps brochures from the Chamber of Commerce, Department of Transportation, AAA, or a city or regional visitors' bureau and pictures from postcards, magazines, and the Internet). Have them cut out pictures related to your state, and invite them to design a collage, paint or color the background, and then paste on their pictures. Older students might create their own individual collage and annotate the pictures with written descriptions to be attached and displayed around the collage.

Making and Using Learning Cards Invite students to draw a picture of a featured item on one index card and write the corresponding label on a second card. (They may reuse any cards they made earlier, adding new ones.) Assist younger, ELL, or struggling students with spelling and writing as necessary. After students have constructed the cards, they can play a matching game by turning over two cards at a time, memorizing the location of matches, and eventually turning over a match (drawn item and written label), and collecting the pair of cards.

Levels of Difficulty

*Easiest, for younger or struggling students and for young English Language Learners (ELLs) and newcomers

**Average difficulty, for older on-grade-level students or more-advanced younger students and for transitioning or mainstreamed English Language Learners (ELLs)

***Most challenging, for above-average, advanced, and gifted students

Creating an Alphabet Book Invite students to construct an alphabet book.

*Younger, ELL, or struggling students could work from their state book to write an alphabet letter on each page and illustrate it. They could do their own version of the illustration or draw an original picture.

/*Older or more advanced students might draw a completely new state-related item for each alphabet letter. Then have them write expository text and/or a verse for each letter.

Making a Diorama or Triorama Invite students to create a diorama or triorama based on one of the state alphabet items (or several related items) in the book. To make a triorama, fold and cut a piece of paper to make a square. Then fold into a triangle, secure, and put a miniature 3-D scene inside. Students may add a description of their scene on an index card.

*Younger, ELL, or struggling students might do a group project based on an alphabet page.

/*Older or more advanced students might do small-group or individual projects that expand on the book illustration(s).

Connecting the Book to Students' Lives

Creating a Family Rhyming Alphabet Book Have students create an illustrated rhyming alphabet book about their own family—including its cultural and personal traditions.

*Younger, ELL, or struggling students might create a class or group book, with an emphasis either on diversity or on similarities and differences.

/*Older or more advanced students might enjoy creating their own book with a four-line rhyme for each alphabet letter and sidebar text that tells more about people, places, events, and traditions significant in their lives.

Levels of Difficulty

*Easiest, for younger or struggling students and for young English Language Learners (ELLs) and newcomers

**Average difficulty, for older on-grade-level students or more-advanced younger students and for transitioning or mainstreamed English Language Learners (ELLs)

***Most challenging, for above-average, advanced, and gifted students

After Reading

Performing the ABCs

*Have younger, ELL, or struggling students put on an alphabet performance. First, allow groups of students to experiment making alphabet shapes with their bodies. Then invite students to choose and read (or memorize and recite) one alphabet letter and to act it out, either by incorporating acting into the reading or by following the reading with an enactment.

**Older or more advanced students might perform the alphabet by doing a group or class program in which each student reads (or recites from memory) one rhyme, followed by a partner who reads the sidebar text and then recites the next rhyme so that students are alternating parts.

***More advanced students might write and perform an alphabet play in which they act out scenes from the book. They might reenact specific events, deliver lines from famous speeches, or do dramatic improvisations.

Levels of Difficulty

*Easiest, for younger or struggling students and for young English Language Learners (ELLs) and newcomers

**Average difficulty, for older on-grade-level students or more-advanced younger students and for transitioning or mainstreamed English Language Learners (ELLs)

***Most challenging, for above-average, advanced, and gifted students

Discover America State by State Teacher's Guide

3. Teaching Special Topic Lessons

Contents

Animals. 16
Arts and Entertainment 20
Cities and Towns 24
Culture and Heritage 28
Ethnic Groups 32
Geography and Climate 36
Government 40
Historical Events 44
Historical Sites and Monuments 48
Natural Attractions 52
Natural Resources 56
People in History 60
Plant Life 64
Sports and Outdoor Activities. 68
State Symbols 72
Technology and Inventions 76
Transportation 80

Animals

What Do Students Know?

Find out what students already know about the state's animals or about a specific creature by asking questions such as the following. If students need help, have them flip through the book as they respond to your prompts. You may choose to create a chart or cluster as students give their responses.

- What are some animals (mammals, birds, fish, reptiles, insects) that live in [state name]?
- Have you seen any of these? Where did you see them? Tell about your experience.
- What is a symbol? (Elicit that it is something that stands for or represents another thing or idea. Examples: The bald eagle is a symbol of the United States and appears on money, stamps, and other items. The dove is a symbol of peace.)

Cross-Curricular Activities

SCIENCE

Identifying Types of Animals *Invite students to help make a chart by paging through their books and pointing out each creature in the illustrations. As they find an example, ask them to identify what kind of animal it is: mammal, fish, bird, reptile, insect, and so on. Write each name under the appropriate column heading, along with a simple drawing or picture.

**Ask students to list other animals in the same general category as the featured one. For example, if the salmon is the featured animal, have students brainstorm a list of different kinds of fish. You may want to sort the animals into those found in your state and those not found or not common to your state. Discuss the different bodies of water in which the fish live (for example, sharks in the ocean and trout in rivers or streams).

Using Scientific Labels *Invite students to describe some of the featured creatures in their book. List the describing words on the board or chart paper. You may wish to draw an outline of the creature and invite students to name the parts (for example, paw, snout, claws, fur, tail, and so on) while you label them.

/*Encourage students to look up the creature in a science or other nonfiction book and/or on the Internet to find its scientific name, as well as more technical terms for labeling features or body parts.

Levels of Difficulty

*Easiest, for younger or struggling students and for young English Language Learners (ELLs) and newcomers

**Average difficulty, for older on-grade-level students or more-advanced younger students and for transitioning or mainstreamed English Language Learners (ELLs)

***Most challenging, for above-average, advanced, and gifted students

LANGUAGE ARTS

Writing an Encyclopedia Entry **/***Have students work in pairs or individually to write brief encyclopedia entries describing some of the featured animals. Invite them to copy their descriptions on cards, omitting the name of the animal. Then have them play a guessing game in which they take turns drawing a card and guessing the creature by its description.

DRAMA, MOVEMENT, AND MUSIC

Imitating Animals *Have students pretend that they are one of the animals in their book. They could make the animal's movements and sounds, use objects in the classroom to construct the animal's habitat, and so on. Others guess what it is. The person who guesses correctly acts out the next creature.

Acting Out Animal Fables **Provide an example of an animal fable (such as why the bear has a short tail). Encourage pairs or small groups of students to plan and act out a known fable or invent a new fable about a creature featured in your state book. Invite them to present their fables to the rest of the class.

GEOGRAPHY AND CLIMATE

Considering Environment *Help students discuss the environment in which the featured animal lives by making connections with your state's geography and climate. Students might want to draw the featured creature in its environment, including the specific geographic features and some indication of climate.

**Students might discuss your state's geography and climate in relation to particular animals' habitats. Encourage students to also consider what characteristics each creature has that make it particularly suited to live in its location and climate.

State to State

Comparing and Contrasting Wildlife Have students select other titles from the *Discover America* series, each student choosing another state or small groups choosing regions of the country very different from their own. Have them compare and contrast some of the wildlife from other parts of the country with that of their state. Encourage them to discuss the relationship between environment and animal life.

Discover America State by State Teacher's Guide

Doing Research Projects

Researching and Reporting on Animals *Invite younger, ELL, or struggling students to choose one characteristic of the animal or its behavior—for example, how the bird builds its nest, how the fish breathes, how an insect protects itself from its enemies, and so on. Provide appropriate research materials for students. Have students tell the group what they learned.

**Invite students, working individually or in pairs, to research the characteristics of a particular class of animals (mammals, reptiles, amphibians, and so on). They could use classroom science books, library materials, or the Internet. Their reports might take the form of a poster presentation, a short paper, an illustrated booklet, or an oral report.

***Have students choose a related topic and explore it in more depth. For example, they could report on several different ways in which animals prepare for winter or survive drought, or on the characteristics and circumstances that have permitted some species to survive while others perish.

Constructing a Nest or Den */**Have students research where a featured bird or animal builds its nest or den (on/under/above the ground, for example) and what materials it uses. Have students use similar (or creative) materials to construct a habitat display in the classroom, including various animals' "homes."

Thinking Critically

Invite students to discuss the featured animals in their state. Some of the following questions might be helpful.

- Why was/were [the featured creature(s)] included in this book?
- [If the featured item is a state symbol] Was/Is the [featured creature] a good choice for our state [animal/bird/fish/insect]? Why or why not? If you had to choose another [animal/bird/fish/insect] as a symbol of our state, which would it be? Why?
- What happens to wildlife when its habitat changes or is destroyed? Give some examples. Is there anything we can do?
- What did you learn that impressed you the most? Why?

Levels of Difficulty

*Easiest, for younger or struggling students and for young English Language Learners (ELLs) and newcomers

**Average difficulty, for older on-grade-level students or more-advanced younger students and for transitioning or mainstreamed English Language Learners (ELLs)

***Most challenging, for above-average, advanced, and gifted students

Extending Knowledge

Reading Independently Have students individually choose a book that includes information about a domestic or wild animal, or other creature of interest. For younger, struggling, or ELL students, provide a selection of library books from which to choose. More proficient readers should visit the library to find a book to read.

Bird Watching *Ask students if they have (or know anyone who has) a birdfeeder at home. Have them find out what kind of feed is in the feeder, and ask them to watch and identify the kinds of birds that come to visit. (If possible, hang a birdfeeder where students can see it to carry out this project at school.) Invite students to name, describe, or draw the birds they see at the feeder.

/*Ask students to watch the feeder for five or ten minutes each day and make a chart or log recording the number and types of birds that visit and any other observations they wish to note.

State to State

Protecting Wildlife Have students check other state books and investigate how states and other agencies protect wildlife, especially endangered species in nature parks, wildlife refuges, aquariums, zoos, and other places, or through special programs, such as repopulation.

Comparing and Contrasting State Symbols Have students compare and contrast several or all the states' animal symbols. Together students might create an illustrated booklet of the state symbols, labeling each page with a state name, writing a sentence or paragraph about each animal, and then arranging their booklet alphabetically by state. If they have chosen more than one type of animal, they could illustrate all the animals of the state on one page. Alternatively, they could create a chart either by state or by animal, noting which states have chosen the same creature. (For example, the mockingbird appears several times.)

Discover America State by State Teacher's Guide

Arts and Entertainment

What Do Students Know?

Explore what students know about the arts and find out about their entertainment interests by asking questions such as the following:

- What kind of art, music, and dance have you done, seen, or heard?
- What kind of art, music, and dance are your favorites?
- What kinds of places do people visit to do or see interesting and entertaining things? (amusement parks, aquariums, circuses, libraries, museums, zoos, and so on) Which of these have you visited?
- Do you know what the term *fine art* means? (art—music, painting, sculpture, and so on—that is made especially for its beauty)

Cross-Curricular Activities

SOCIAL STUDIES

Exploring the Arts, Culture, and Entertainment *Have students page through the state alphabet book, looking for any and all forms of the arts, culture, and entertainment (art, dance, music; places such as aquariums, circuses, libraries, museums, zoos, and so on). Make a chart or a web on the chalkboard, organizing students' responses into categories.

/*Ask students why people make art, compose music, create dances, or perform in plays. Help students understand that we share customs, stories, and values through these art forms. We also express ideas about beauty through visual and performing arts.

LANGUAGE ARTS

Using Descriptive Words Invite students to look through the book for an exciting example of art, music, dance, or entertainment. *Have younger, ELL, or struggling students describe the illustration. Provide vocabulary help, as needed. Ask students to then dictate or write two words that describe the illustration. They might use words such as *loud* or *tiny* to describe how something sounds or looks, and they might also describe their feelings about it, using words like *beautiful* or *fun*. Provide spelling help as necessary.

/*Ask older or more advanced students to write a sentence or two, or even a paragraph, describing the example they have chosen, paying particular attention to descriptive words and phrases.

Levels of Difficulty

*Easiest, for younger or struggling students and for young English Language Learners (ELLs) and newcomers

**Average difficulty, for older on-grade-level students or more-advanced younger students and for transitioning or mainstreamed English Language Learners (ELLs)

***Most challenging, for above-average, advanced, and gifted students

Writing a Poem **/***Invite students to compose a diamante about an art form or a place of entertainment. A diamante is a seven-line poem in the shape of a diamond. Each line uses a specific part of speech. You may wish to display the structure of a diamante on the board and an example such as the following:

Line 1: one noun/ Line 2: two adjectives/ Line 3: three -ing verbs/ Line 4: four nouns/ Line 5: three -ing verbs/ Line 6: two adjectives/ Line 7: one noun

circus
noisy, huge
laughing, clowning, swinging
big top, trapeze, elephants, lion tamer
performing, balancing, clapping
tricky, colorful
spectacle

Invite volunteers to read their poems to the class. You might want to create a display of the completed diamantes.

Drama, Movement, and Music

Exploring Creative Expression and Rhythm Provide students with simple percussion instruments, such as triangles, wood blocks, or drums. (Alternatively, students can use classroom items, such as rulers or pencils, to make percussive sounds.) Invite students to create a rhythm that reminds them of one place that the class or group has discussed. (A fast rhythm might represent a circus, for example; a slower rhythm might represent a museum.) Invite volunteers to share their rhythms with the class.

Composing a Jingle ***Ask students to identify an arts or entertainment location in your state. Challenge them to write a jingle to advertise the place they have chosen. Encourage students to create a catchy tune and rhyming lyrics that are easy to remember. In the jingle, they should include one or two important descriptions of the place. If possible, provide students with recording devices and allow them to record their jingles.

Discover America State by State Teacher's Guide

Doing Research Projects

Researching a Museum, Library, or Place of Entertainment
Have students find out more about a museum, library, or place of entertainment mentioned in your state book. Provide on-level materials, as well as pamphlets and brochures from the organization, if possible, and/or have students visit the organization's Web site. *Ask younger, ELL, or struggling students to tell about what they found.

**Older or more advanced students might work individually, in pairs, or in small groups to compile a list of exhibits, resources, or entertainment features of the organization.

Researching Arts and Crafts **/***Invite students to learn about the history of arts and crafts in your state. (Art forms might include visual or performing arts; crafts might include quilting, pottery, jewelry-making, and so on.) Students should choose one craft or art form for their research. Encourage them to use textbooks, library resources, or the Internet to gather information and to illustrate or demonstrate what they learn. In their report, students might address the following questions about the art or craft: Who practiced it first? What materials are needed? How has the art form or craft changed over the years? Where can people go to see it? Invite students to give an oral presentation or a demonstration to the class.

Thinking Critically

You might want to use questions such as the following to help students think more critically about art and entertainment.

- What is art? What is "good art"? What is "bad art"? "good music"? "bad music"? Is there such a thing?
- Are there examples of art that are not found in museums? (street art, murals on the outside of buildings, graffiti)
- Are some places where people go for entertainment "better" than others? Which places? Why are they better?

Levels of Difficulty

*Easiest, for younger or struggling students and for young English Language Learners (ELLs) and newcomers

**Average difficulty, for older on-grade-level students or more-advanced younger students and for transitioning or mainstreamed English Language Learners (ELLs)

***Most challenging, for above-average, advanced, and gifted students

State to State

Combining Geography and Math Have students browse through other titles from the *Discover America* series to find the most entertaining spots in the United States. Provide students with a map that includes a scale and have them mark the location of each spot. Then ask students to create a plan for a summer driving trip that begins in their home state and includes at least four of their favorite locations. Have students plan the route and determine how far they must travel. For an added challenge, suggest that students determine how to go to all four locations and travel the least number of miles on the trip.

Extending Knowledge

Visiting an Art Museum Arrange a trip to a local art museum. If possible, have a guide take students on a tour. Have students take along a pencil and a sketchbook or notebook, and encourage them to sketch pieces of art that they find appealing. Ask them to record the title of the artwork and the artist. After the visit, invite volunteers to describe their favorite piece of art and to show their sketches to the class.

Designing a Cultural Arts and Entertainment Center Provide students with graph paper, rulers, and pencils, and ask them to design a new cultural arts and entertainment center for their area. Remind them to think about the arts and entertainment that are representative of your region. Encourage students to brainstorm about what they might include in the center, such as a stage or a museum space. Have them sketch and label their designs on the graph paper. Then display the designs around the classroom.

Reading Independently Invite students to read a biography about a famous artist, musician, or dancer; if feasible, encourage them to choose someone from your state. Have a sufficient number of appropriate-level books so that younger, ELL, and struggling students have plenty of choices. More advanced students can get the books from the school or public library. Suggest that students give a brief report about the biography; interested students can pretend to be the person as they give details about his or her life.

State to State

Making and Playing an Arts and Entertainment Memory Game Have each student choose a title from the *Discover America* series and find an artist, an art form, or a place to experience the arts or entertainment. Students should write the name on one index card; on a second card, have them write the name of the state. Give them a chance to present their two cards to the other players. Then gather twelve pairs of cards and place the cards upside down so they form a square. Have students choose a partner and play the memory-matching game. One person turns over two cards. If the name of the artist, art form, or place belongs in the state, the player gets to keep the pair of cards. Players should take turns trying to make matches until all matches have been made.

Discover America State by State Teacher's Guide

Cities and Towns

What Do Students Know?

Find out what students already know about the featured city or town by asking questions such as the following:

- Have you ever been to [city/town name]? Tell about your experiences.
- Do you know in which part of the state [city/town name] is located? Where is it?
- Do you know why it is famous? Explain.
- Do you know of any famous buildings or monuments there? Tell about them.

Cross-Curricular Activities

SOCIAL STUDIES

Identifying Services Have students brainstorm a list of city, state, and federal services in the city or town. (These might include schools, libraries, police, post office, firefighters, garbage collection, street cleaning, playgrounds and parks, lighting, road repair, and so on.)

*Younger, ELL, or struggling students might make a drawing or poster that depicts one of these services. Lead a discussion about how people depend on each other.

/*Older or more advanced students might try to specify under which of three categories (city, state, federal) each service belongs. You might want to record the list in columns on the chalkboard or on poster board and display it.

Levels of Difficulty

*Easiest, for younger or struggling students and for young English Language Learners (ELLs) and newcomers

**Average difficulty, for older on-grade-level students or more-advanced younger students and for transitioning or mainstreamed English Language Learners (ELLs)

***Most challenging, for above-average, advanced, and gifted students

State to State

Exploring Modes of Transportation Have each student consult one or more books in the *Discover America* series to find modes of transportation in cities and towns of other states. Some students may use the Index at the back of this Teacher's Guide in their search. Using prior knowledge and what they learned from the state histories, have students make a chart showing which cities use the various modes of transportation. Discuss why cities developed particular transportation modes. Ask why some cities have extensive public transportation systems and others don't. The chart and discussion could also revolve around changes in the modes of transportation from 1776 to the present.

Talking About Transportation Have students discuss ways of getting around the city or town (cars, bikes, buses, trains, taxis, subways, trolleys, and so on).

*Younger, ELL, or struggling students might make a drawing that depicts one mode of transportation. Have them label the drawing and dictate or write a sentence about it.

/*Older or more advanced students might discuss the agency/organization responsible for each mode of transportation.

Finding Things to Do Help students name things to do for fun in the city or town. Make a list on the chalkboard and add a symbol to represent each choice (for example, a stick figure, a tree, or a baseball). Older or more advanced students might write accompanying descriptions of each attraction.

Geography

Making a City Map Give students an outline map of the city or town. Depending on the map (and if possible), help students indicate or locate their school and a few familiar streets.

*Younger, ELL, or struggling students might color the map, cut it out, and paste it into a scrapbook of other state-related maps and drawings.

**Older or more advanced students might fill in as many streets and landmarks as they can.

Doing Research Projects

Gathering Information *Have younger, ELL, or struggling students talk to parents, guardians, older siblings, or other adults about all the different people who help run a city or town, such as police officers, firefighters, or sanitation workers. Have students share their findings with the class.

Reporting on the City or Town **/***Have older or more advanced students do research to find out where the city or town gets what it needs. For example, where do food and water come from? Where does gas and electricity come from? How do goods get into the city? How does sewage get out? Encourage students to get help from librarians and/or other people in the city or town. The product could take the form of a poster presentation, a short paper, an illustrated booklet, or an oral report.

Discover America State by State Teacher's Guide

Reporting on the State Capital ******Have older or more advanced students find out more about the state capital by doing research and collecting data. Encourage them to use reference books, nonfiction books, magazines, the Internet, and so on. The report could take the form of a poster presentation, a short paper, or an illustrated booklet.

Creating a Time Line *******Have students make a time line or a chart showing what was occurring at the time the city became the state capital. What was happening politically, culturally, nationally? What were the important issues?

Art/Architecture

Building Projects Have each student choose a building that is either well known or typical of a particular area or neighborhood (from skyscraper to bungalow).

Making a Model *****Younger, ELL, or struggling students might make a drawing or model of the building or even construct a neighborhood out of empty boxes, cans, and other items.

Planning a City ****/*****Older or more advanced students might design a new city, working on a large sheet of poster board. Encourage students to create streets with residential, business, service, cultural, and recreational buildings of their choice.

Thinking Critically

Invite students to discuss the city or town, using questions such as the following:

- What makes [name of city or town] a good place to live? Why?
- What are some of the best things about the town/city?
- What problems are there? (pollution/overcrowding/inadequate services, for example)
- Who is a well-known person from [name of place]? What qualities make [name of person] well known?

Levels of Difficulty

*Easiest, for younger or struggling students and for young English Language Learners (ELLs) and newcomers

**Average difficulty, for older on-grade-level students or more-advanced younger students and for transitioning or mainstreamed English Language Learners (ELLs)

***Most challenging, for above-average, advanced, and gifted students

State to State

Learning About State Capitals Encourage students to use the books of the *Discover America* series to learn about the state capitals of all fifty states as well as about our nation's capital, the District of Columbia. Older students may supplement this information with other research. *****Some students may create a state capitals map by locating and labeling capital cities on an outline map. ****/*****Other students may prepare reports on different capital cities or on the construction and features of various capitol buildings, gathering images from the Internet to illustrate their written, computer-generated, or oral reports.

Extending Knowledge

Reading Independently Have students individually locate an encyclopedia or magazine article about the city. For younger, ELL, or struggling students, provide encyclopedias, magazines, or Internet sites. More competent readers should visit the library to find an article. Have students tell about their articles in discussion groups.

Touring Your City Arrange for interested groups of students or the whole class to take a tour of your town or city, to visit some municipal buildings, and, if possible, to see some city or state officials. Gear the outing to students' special interests, such as architecture, a particular transportation system, a service (fire fighting or animal control, for example). Help them prepare for the tour and provide ways of sharing what they learned.

State to State

Studying Buildings and Landmarks Encourage students to use the *Discover America* series to find out about other buildings and landmarks around the United States. In addition to comparing buildings—for example, those in Mystic Village in Connecticut and in Walt Disney World in Florida—they may also research and compare famous landmarks, such as the Arch in Missouri, the Brooklyn Bridge in New York, Mount Rushmore in South Dakota, the Space Needle in Washington State, the Watts Towers in California, and so on. You may also wish students to research and compare historical landmarks such as Fort Ticonderoga in New York, the Old North Church in Massachusetts, St. Augustine in Florida, or Tombstone in Arizona.

Culture and Heritage

What Do Students Know?

Help students understand the concept of culture and its influence on our lives by having them talk about their family's heritage. As a class, you might draw a cluster or concept map on chart paper like the one below. ***** Simplify the web for younger students. Then add new ideas and examples throughout the lesson.

/* Older, more advanced, and gifted students may create a fairly elaborate concept map. Encourage them to include ideas about beliefs, dialects, and folklore, and to add new ideas during their study of the lesson.

Concept map with **Culture** at center, connected to:
- food and cooking
- national origin: where family/relatives came from
- languages
- religion and beliefs
- holidays and celebrations: New Year's Day, birthdays, weddings
- folk dances, traditional music
- clothing and costumes
- games and entertainment
- arts and crafts

- Lead students to conclude that *culture* means the ideas, customs, arts, traditions, language, and beliefs that make up the way a group of people live and that are passed down from generation to generation.
- What are some examples of your family's culture? Invite students to share information in each of the web categories. Does anyone in your family speak another language? How does your family celebrate birthdays or New Year's Day? Is there a special music you play at family gatherings?

Levels of Difficulty

* Easiest, for younger or struggling students and for young English Language Learners (ELLs) and newcomers

** Average difficulty, for older on-grade-level students or more-advanced younger students and for transitioning or mainstreamed English Language Learners (ELLs)

*** Most challenging, for above-average, advanced, and gifted students

Special Topic: Culture and Heritage

Cross-Curricular Activities

SOCIAL STUDIES

Making a Visual *Have students page through their books as you help them find some examples of your state's culture and heritage, including objects, songs, dances, clothing, arts, crafts, food, and celebrations. Sort the examples with the class into categories in a chart or table.

/*Ask students to record examples, information, and pictures on a concept map like the one created for their family culture or in a computer slide show.

Sharing Pieces of the Past Have students ask their parents, aunts, uncles, and grandparents about their family history and culture. Invite students to bring copies of old photos and stories about special items that have been passed down in their family for many years (such as a ring, a watch, a piece of furniture, or a book). Invite volunteers to share the story of such an item: Where did it come from? How did someone save it or come to own it?

LANGUAGE ARTS

Discovering the Origin of Names */**Invite students to look for labels, titles, and names in your state and local area that are taken from different cultures. Which are names of famous people? What do some of the names mean and what language are they from? Encourage students to look at names of streets, businesses, parks, schools, and other buildings, as well as brand names of local products.

Discussing Folk Literature Select a folk tale or legend from another culture in your state (for example, Native American, African, Spanish, English, German, Cajun) and read it aloud to the class. Encourage students to discuss the beliefs, customs, and traditions of each culture. Supply your classroom library or reading center with additional folk literature of various reading levels.

Cultural Collage */**Have students work in pairs or small groups to choose one topic related to your state culture, such as arts and crafts, clothing, customs, celebrations, holidays, languages, food, dances, or types of music. Provide students with newspapers, Internet sites, and magazines to use for making a cultural collage.

***More advanced and gifted students might work independently and make a collage on more than one topic.

Discover America State by State Teacher's Guide

Recording Celebrations and Holidays Create a calendar of special occasions. Include personal holidays, such as birthdays. Encourage the class to brainstorm other holidays and record them on a large calendar. Have them distinguish between state holidays, such as your state independence day, and national holidays, such as the Fourth of July. If there is time, students can add symbols and illustrations.

Doing Research Projects

Researching Cultural Influences Encourage students to conduct further research on another culture in their state and learn how it influenced life in the past and continues to influence the state today. Have students pick two or three categories such as food and clothing, or music and art. They may use classroom textbooks, library resources, or the Internet. Suggest they give a short presentation or demonstration in which they wear elements of the traditional dress of the chosen culture, display photos or objects, and talk about what they learned. ****/*****More advanced and gifted students could summarize their research in a three- to five-page research paper or computer slide show.

Thinking Critically

Encourage a discussion about culture and heritage. Some of the following questions may be useful.

- What are some changes in the way we live today compared with when your parents were growing up? How has culture changed with respect to clothing, meals, and attitudes?
- What do you like about your family's culture? What do you like about being American?
- How would our lives be if everyone were exactly the same?
- What happens to our community when people do not respect and try to understand each other's cultures?

State to State

Recording Holidays Divide students into groups, and ask them to use the *Discover America* series to complete a celebration and holiday calendar for the United States. Younger and struggling students may complete the calendar in several steps with your help. More advanced students might complete the activity independently in their groups.

Recognizing American Pop Culture Encourage students to use other titles in the *Discover America* series, as well as other resources including books, magazines, newspapers, and the Internet, to make a collage about American popular culture. Discuss that typically "American" items such as blue jeans, hamburgers and French fries, and rock 'n' roll music are all a part of American pop culture, which influences other cultures around the world.

Levels of Difficulty

*Easiest, for younger or struggling students and for young English Language Learners (ELLs) and newcomers

**Average difficulty, for older on-grade-level students or more-advanced younger students and for transitioning or mainstreamed English Language Learners (ELLs)

***Most challenging, for above-average, advanced, and gifted students

Special Topic: Culture and Heritage

Extending Knowledge

Experiencing Festivals Provide students and their families with information about local festivals, street fairs, and cultural events, including those given by churches with ethnic congregations. When students attend such an event, invite them to share their new experiences: foods, music, games, handicrafts.

Learning About Other Cultures Invite parents and other guest speakers from various cultures to speak to the class about their heritage, customs, and cultural similarities and differences. Encourage students to ask questions.

Exchanging Recipes Invite parents and students to bring a traditional recipe and/or food item from their family's culture. Discuss how food and customs surrounding eating are an important part of people's heritage. Have families label their dishes in their language and, if possible, in English.

/*Point out that a recipe is written to provide instructions for making something. Ask students to write a recipe or directions for how to make their favorite food or baked good, including ingredients, procedure, and helpful tips. Remind them to write steps in the correct order and to use time order words such as *first, next, then, after,* and *before.*

State to State

Appreciating Culture Through Music Invite students to bring to class samples of music representative of the different countries and ethnic groups that make up the United States, as well as music that originated in the United States (country, blues, jazz, bluegrass, and rock 'n' roll). Encourage students to look at other books from the *Discover America* series. Ask them to identify where the music may have come from. They may also try to identify the musical instruments they hear, and clap or move to the rhythm or beat of the music.

Celebrating Other Cultures During the year, select one or two holidays widely celebrated but associated with a particular culture or ethnic group (for example, St. Patrick's Day, Cinco de Mayo, or Chinese New Year). Have students learn about the holiday and why and how it is celebrated. Invite them to make decorations, bring food, play music, perform dances, make arts and crafts, and wear clothing that would be appropriate for that celebration.

Discover America State by State Teacher's Guide

Ethnic Groups

What Do Students Know?

Find out what students understand by the term *ethnic group* and what they already know about specific groups by asking questions such as the following:

- What is an ethnic group? (term refers to people who share a special cultural, national, racial, or religious background)
- What ethnic groups can you think of? (African Americans; Amish people; Hispanic people; Native Americans; various Caucasian European or Asian nationalities)
- What ethnic group are you a member of?
- What is special about your ethnic group?

Cross-Curricular Activities

SOCIAL STUDIES

Talking About an Ethnic Group *Have students look at the illustration related to the featured ethnic group. Ask younger, ELL, or struggling students what they can learn about the group from the picture. You might want to make a web on the board as students respond.

**Ask older or more advanced students to work in pairs or in small groups to write a list of words or phrases that describe the ethnic group, using the verse, the sidebar, and the illustration. Invite a volunteer from each group to share the list. Did any groups come up with some of the same words and phrases?

Exploring the Culture *Have students identify objects associated with the group (food, homes, tools, vehicles) as well as occupations, recreation, and so on. Then have students close their book while a volunteer makes a quick sketch on the board. Ask students to guess which object or aspect of life is being depicted.

/*After older or more advanced students have identified objects, occupations, and so on, divide students into teams. Without looking at their books, the first student on Team A names a category, such as *food*. Any member of Team B responds with the specific food. Then Team B names the category, and Team A responds. Teams get a point for each correct answer.

Levels of Difficulty

*Easiest, for younger or struggling students and for young English Language Learners (ELLs) and newcomers

**Average difficulty, for older on-grade-level students or more-advanced younger students and for transitioning or mainstreamed English Language Learners (ELLs)

***Most challenging, for above-average, advanced, and gifted students

LANGUAGE ARTS

Creating a Sequence *Depending on the featured ethnic group, help students make up a short story or description that orders events in a sequence. For an ethnic group that plants, for example, you might draw stick figures on the board, mixing up the sequence of someone planting seeds, watering young plants, picking the plants, and cooking the plants. Invite students to tell the story in the correct sequence. You might then want to write the appropriate sentence under each picture on the board and encourage students to copy the sentences, arranging them in the correct sequence.

/*Ask older or more advanced students, working individually or in pairs, to create their own story sequence. If necessary, begin by having the group as a whole brainstorm topics, such as planting, building a home, traveling on water, and so on. Have students write the story sequence individually, and encourage them to use time-order words such as *First, Next, Then*, and so on. Students might illustrate their sequence with stick figures.

Doing Research Projects

Researching Ethnic Groups *Help students identify something about the ethnic group they would like to learn more about (history, vehicles, other locations). Provide appropriate materials from the library or the Internet. Encourage students to make sketches or help them jot down notes. Have students take turns in a group discussion, showing and telling about what they learned.

/*Encourage older or more advanced students to do research on another ethnic group in your state. Provide history books, reference materials, library materials, and/or Internet information to help students identify new groups. Invite students to present their research as a written report, a poster presentation, or an illustrated booklet.

State to State

Comparing and Contrasting Ethnic Groups Invite students to browse through several titles in the *Discover America* series to find one or more other ethnic groups. Invite students to compare and contrast the groups. Younger, ELL, and struggling students might work as a class with you; older or more advanced students might work individually, in pairs, or in small groups. Have students make a chart with column headings such as *Clothing, Homes, Jobs, Tools*, and so on. Students might enjoy illustrating their charts.

Constructing Homes Have students page through titles in the *Discover America* series or help them go online to locate pictures of the kinds of homes built by different ethnic groups. Divide students into groups and provide them with natural or creative materials to build homes that are in some way similar to the homes they learned about.

Thinking Critically

Encourage students to think more deeply about ethnic groups by asking questions such as the following:

- How did each ethnic group you studied contribute to life in the United States?
- Do you know any ways in which specific ethnic groups have suffered in the past? What happened?
- If what happened to a particular ethnic group was the result of an act of the U.S. government, was the government honoring the laws and ideals of the United States?
- Do you know if any ethnic groups are still suffering today? If so, how? How could the situation be improved?
- Do you think money has anything to do with how specific ethnic groups or certain members of those groups are treated? Explain.

Extending Knowledge

Reading Legends Read to students one or more legends from one or more ethnic groups. (There are many legends on the Internet that are one page or shorter.) If you choose two or more legends that explain something in nature, such as why the sun rises or why an animal looks or acts the way it does, you could then encourage students to compare and contrast the legends.

Reading Biographies *Provide appropriate level biographies or biographical articles about people from specific ethnic groups who were famous long ago and who are famous today. You might read excerpts to pique students' interest. Encourage younger, ELL, or struggling students to discuss the accomplishments they learn about.

/*Encourage older or more advanced students to read about two figures in the same ethnic group, someone from the past and someone today. Invite them to compare and contrast the accomplishments of both figures.

Levels of Difficulty

*Easiest, for younger or struggling students and for young English Language Learners (ELLs) and newcomers

**Average difficulty, for older on-grade-level students or more-advanced younger students and for transitioning or mainstreamed English Language Learners (ELLs)

***Most challenging, for above-average, advanced, and gifted students

Doing Arts and Crafts Provide materials and appropriate level reference books to help students create artwork representative of an ethnic group they studied. Students might paint pottery, make jewelry, design a blanket, and so on.

Learning Through Art From a library, get art books with paintings of Native Americans in the American West, including those painted by Charles Russell, who had a very sympathetic view. Have students comment on what they can learn from the paintings about Native American life during that period of time (dress, family life, hunting, relationship to nature, and so on). If you locate modern paintings, discuss how they contrast with the earlier ones.

State to State

Identifying Native American Place Names Explain that many states, cities, towns, and streets in the United States have Native American names. Using a map of your state (or a local map, if appropriate), have students speculate about which names might be Native American. Expand this activity to other states. You might start with considering the names of individual states.

Finding Native American Populations Have students browse through titles in the *Discover America* series to find states in different regions with Native American populations. Students might create a population map, showing major locations of different Native American groups.

Exploring Ethnic Celebrations Encourage students to use your state book and other titles in the *Discover America* series to explore how different ethnic groups celebrate their traditions. Have students locate different kinds of cultural artwork and activities—art, dance, legends, music, poems, and so on. Students could compare and contrast these, or they might learn some poems, stories, or songs to recite or perform.

Geography and Climate

What Do Students Know?

Encourage students to share information about your state's geography and climate. Find out what they already know by asking questions such as the following:

- What does *geography* mean? (the study of the earth and its features, including mountains, valleys, deserts, beaches, oceans, rivers, and so on)
- What do you know about the geography of [state name]?
- What does *climate* mean? (Encourage students to include not only weather and temperature but also precipitation, wind, likelihood of storms, and so on.)
- What is the climate in our state? (Clarify climate versus season, if necessary.)

Cross-Curricular Activities

Math

Reading Weather Maps and Forecasts Provide students with a local newspaper clipping or display an Internet site that shows a weather map. Have students look at the daily forecast and discuss the graphics used to predict weather, temperature, rainfall, and so on. (Draw their attention to color coding, abbreviations, and symbols.)

*Invite students to create cards with symbols (sun, clouds, snowflake, etc.) used in the forecasts. Then, have them play a game in which they draw a card and tell what it means.

/*Have students look at the forecast for the next few days. Invite them to notice patterns in the information and numbers. Then have them add or subtract predicted temperatures to tell the difference in degrees predicted for each day.

Levels of Difficulty

*Easiest, for younger or struggling students and for young English Language Learners (ELLs) and newcomers

**Average difficulty, for older on-grade-level students or more-advanced younger students and for transitioning or mainstreamed English Language Learners (ELLs)

***Most challenging, for above-average, advanced, and gifted students

State to State

Comparing U.S. Geography and Weather Display a topographic map of the United States and engage students in a discussion about geographic features of different regions. Then provide a current weather map of the country and have students relate weather conditions to geography.

SCIENCE/SOCIAL STUDIES

Connecting Geography and Climate */**Show students a globe, and help a volunteer locate your state. Have students locate the equator, and then guide a discussion that includes the information that locations closer to the equator have warmer climates while places farther from the equator have colder climates. Also, talk about the moderate climates on the coasts and near the Great Lakes in the United States. Discuss the effects of altitude on temperature. (Temperatures are lower at higher altitudes; temperatures are higher at lower altitudes.)

***Encourage students to draw conclusions about other factors that influence your state's climate and weather. (States near the ocean are more likely to have hurricanes and/or tropical storms. Locations closer to the equator have less difference from season to season; areas farther away from the equator have fewer daylight hours throughout the year, and so on.)

Using Maps and Models *Invite students to look through their books for examples of landforms and bodies of water. Then have them brainstorm a list of different forms (deserts, plains, valleys, mountains, volcanoes, beaches, rivers, oceans, bays, and so on). You might want to have younger, ELL, or struggling students choose two or three landforms or bodies of water to draw and label.

**Provide each student with a physical map of your state. Have students color and label the landforms and bodies of water, using terms like *desert, plains, valley, mountain, volcano, beach, plateau, island, peninsula, bay, river, lake*, and so on.

***Invite advanced students to create a physical map that shows the geography of the state, including landforms. Encourage them to label the geographic features on the map itself or in a key.

State to State

Comparing Geographical Features Have each student choose a title in the *Discover America* series and identify landforms and bodies of water in another state. Invite students to discuss the similarities and differences between the states, or to make a chart comparing and contrasting their landforms and/or bodies of water. Advanced students might create a physical map of the state, and compare it with the one they made of their own state.

Discover America State by State Teacher's Guide

Doing Research Projects

Researching Geography and Climate *Invite younger, ELL, or struggling students to choose one landform (mountains, beaches, valleys, plateaus, deserts, plains, etc.). Provide on-level library books, encyclopedias, and other resources for students to find information. Have students find a picture of their landform and orally present what they learned about it (what it looks like, how it is formed, where it is normally found, and so on).

**Ask older or more advanced students to conduct research on a natural disaster or severe weather condition in your state. Encourage them to use textbooks, library resources, or the Internet for information. Invite them to share their research through a poster presentation, a mock news report, or an oral or written report.

***Invite gifted and advanced students to research a specific natural disaster or natural wonder in your state. Encourage them to include background information and to make connections to geography and climate. Have students present their research in a written report, a travel brochure, or a computer slide show.

Thinking Critically

Invite students to discuss what they have learned about geography and climate. Some of the following questions might be helpful:

- What did you learn about geography and climate that you didn't know before?
- How are geography and climate related in [state name]?
- Why do some states have more severe weather (hurricanes, tornadoes, thunderstorms) than others?
- Name other things that geography and climate influence, particularly what they affected in the past (where cities were built, what houses were made of, communications, what people could grow and had to eat, and so on).

Levels of Difficulty

*Easiest, for younger or struggling students and for young English Language Learners (ELLs) and newcomers

**Average difficulty, for older on-grade-level students or more-advanced younger students and for transitioning or mainstreamed English Language Learners (ELLs)

***Most challenging, for above-average, advanced, and gifted students

Extending Knowledge

Looking at Landscapes Encourage students to examine pictures, photographs, or paintings of landscapes they have never seen. For younger, ELL, or struggling students, provide a selection of art or travel books, calendar art, and other pictures. Intermediate and advanced students could collect their own pictures from books, magazines, newspapers, or the Internet. Encourage them to discuss and display their impressions and findings.

Visiting a TV station Arrange to visit a local television station to learn how it forecasts the weather each day. Help students prepare a few questions to ask TV staff members. If possible, obtain permission for students to see equipment, maps, tools, etc., involved in predicting weather. When students return to the classroom, encourage them to discuss what they learned.

Graphing Weather Forecasts Invite students to use a newspaper or the Internet to find information about the weather in their city or town. Have them create a graph based on the information.

*Have younger, ELL, or struggling students make a bar graph to record the high temperature for three days. They might work as a large group or in several small groups.

**Encourage older or advanced students to create bar graphs for the high and low temperatures in their area and an area with a different climate for one week.

***Challenge gifted or more advanced students to use high and low temperatures to calculate average temperatures in their state. Have them create a bar or line graph that shows low, high, and average temperatures for each month of the year. Then they could calculate the high, low, and average temperatures for the year.

State to State

Playing a Quiz Game Have students select titles from the *Discover America* series to find information about the geography and climate of other states. Invite them to copy information about the climate and geography on one side of a card and to write the name of the state on the other side. Students take turns reading their descriptions aloud, making sure to cover the name of the state on the back of the card. The person who correctly guesses the state could take the next turn, or you may wish to call on volunteers instead.

Discover America State by State Teacher's Guide

Government

What Do Students Know?

Find out what students know about government by asking questions such as the following:

- Who is the president of the United States? Who is the governor of [your state name]?
- How does someone become president or governor?
- Where is our state capitol building? Have you visited it?
- What is a law? What are some laws or rules you have at home and at school? What are some laws the government has? (traffic laws, for example)
- Do you know the name of any writing (documents) about our country's government or laws? (Declaration of Independence, Constitution, Bill of Rights, etc.)

Cross-Curricular Activities

Social Studies

Identifying Political Figures *Invite students to brainstorm a list of political figures they know by name or by title. Record their responses on the board, including each person's title and name, if known.

**Encourage older or more advanced students to help you create a chart with column titles (President, Vice President, Cabinet Members, Senators, and so on). Encourage students to think about state and local politicians in addition to national figures.

Understanding the Branches of Government Tell students, or elicit from them, that state government has three branches. One branch makes and writes laws (legislative), another decides if laws are fair or broken (judicial), and the last branch leads the state (executive).

*Provide index cards for each branch and the people related to each one (for example, governor, House of Representatives and Senate, and judges). Assist students in arranging the cards in a mobile showing the basic organization of state government.

/*Ask students to create a chart or table with columns for the three branches of government. Have them label rows for different jobs or positions in state government, including governor, lieutenant governor, House of Representatives, Senate, and judges. Discuss the duties of each office and whether each official is elected or appointed.

Levels of Difficulty

*Easiest, for younger or struggling students and for young English Language Learners (ELLs) and newcomers

**Average difficulty, for older on-grade-level students or more-advanced younger students and for transitioning or mainstreamed English Language Learners (ELLs)

***Most challenging, for above-average, advanced, and gifted students

Deciding Who Makes Laws Discuss the U.S. Congress (Senate and House of Representatives) and what it does (makes laws for the whole country). Also discuss your state government and what it does (makes laws for the state). Then give students examples such as the following, and ask whether the U.S. government or the state government would make the laws in each instance: how many days you go to school every year, how the post office is run, whether a certain day will be a national holiday.

LANGUAGE ARTS

Discussing School Issues *Explain to students that political candidates often debate topics so that people can know their opinion and what they plan to do if elected. Invite students to discuss an issue that might be appropriately debated in your school: school opening hours, dress code, sale of certain types of food, additional recess time, and so on. Encourage students to discuss the pros and cons while you record their responses on the board.

/*Invite volunteers to develop more fully their arguments for or against and stage a debate on one or more of the issues.

Being a Good Citizen *Invite students to explore the rights and responsibilities of U.S. citizens. First, elicit that a citizen is a member of a country. Then discuss how one becomes a citizen of the United States. Invite younger, ELL, or struggling students to brainstorm a list and help make a chart about the rights and responsibilities of citizens. (Rights include freedom of speech, of religion, of the press; the right to assemble, to have a trial by jury, to vote, to run for public office. Responsibilities include obeying laws, paying taxes, voting, serving on a jury if called, being informed about public issues.)

/*After students have discussed the topic and brainstormed the list, invite more advanced students to write a paragraph or a short essay on the rights and responsibilities of a good citizen.

State to State

Finding Information About Historical Documents Give small groups of students four to six titles from the *Discover America* series. Invite them to find any information they can about historical documents. Have each group prepare a list of each document it found and note which state book told about it. Then have students compare information to see if the same document was mentioned in more than one state book.

Doing Research Projects

Researching and Reporting on Government *Provide appropriate-level newspaper or magazine materials, or have students get help from adults at home. Have younger, ELL, or struggling students find and cut out headlines, photos, and articles related to the federal or your state government. They could paste their clippings onto one of two poster boards, which you have labeled Federal Government and State Government, respectively.

/*Invite older or more advanced students to work individually or in pairs to research and report in more detail on either the functions of one of the three branches of the federal government or on a person in one of those branches. The report might take the form of a poster presentation, a short written paper, an illustrated booklet, or an oral report.

Checking Out State Government Web Sites Find and then direct students to a Web site for information about state government. Your own state government Web site might have a children's page, or you might try a search on the Internet.

Thinking Critically

Invite students to reflect on the significance of what they have been learning by asking questions such as the following:

- Why do we need laws? What would happen if we didn't have laws?
- Do you think that laws are always "fair" to everyone? Can a law be "just" and still not satisfy the wishes of some individuals or groups? Explain your answer.
- Do you think you would like to be a politician, a judge, or other state official? Why or why not?
- Have you learned or been told that the government of the United States is different from the governments in many other countries of the world? How is it different?

Levels of Difficulty

*Easiest, for younger or struggling students and for young English Language Learners (ELLs) and newcomers

**Average difficulty, for older on-grade-level students or more-advanced younger students and for transitioning or mainstreamed English Language Learners (ELLs)

***Most challenging, for above-average, advanced, and gifted students

State to State

Exploring Relationships Among Government, State Laws, and State Organizations Have students page through other titles in the *Discover America* series for information related to the U.S. government, state laws, and state organizations. Have them use sticky notes to mark the pages they find. Then have volunteers, working as a class or in small groups, read aloud a verse or some of the sidebar information. Provide reading help as necessary. Have students discuss similarities and differences between any aspect they find of the federal and the state governments of different states.

Special Topic: Government

Extending Knowledge

Reciting from a Famous Document *Using information from a history book or the Internet, guide a discussion about a famous document (Bill of Rights, Constitution, Declaration of Independence, Emancipation Proclamation, Gettysburg Address, Bill of Rights). Read a famous line or phrase from that document, write it on the board, and have students recite it with you.

/*Invite older or more advanced students to choose a longer segment of a famous document and copy it. Encourage them to practice reading their quotation or memorize it if they wish. Then have volunteers take turns giving a dramatic reading or recitation for the class.

Visiting a Government Building Arrange to have students visit your state capitol building or town hall. Prepare and photocopy questions for them to answer during and/or after the trip. When you return, invite students to discuss the trip and write a class or individual thank-you letter to tell what they learned or enjoyed the most.

Finding Out More About Government Invite students to find out more about any document, government agency, or law that interests them. Provide appropriate level information for younger, ELL, or struggling students. More competent readers can use the library or the Internet to find information.

Writing to a Representative Challenge students to pick a cause or subject they feel strongly about, such as more money or resources for schools, parks, or bicycle lanes. Encourage them to write a letter to a state representative telling why the representative should support the cause.

State to State

Comparing and Contrasting State Capitol Buildings Have students page through other titles in the *Discover America* series for information about state capitol buildings. Younger, ELL, or struggling students could help you make a chart listing the state, the location of the capitol building, and a description of it. Older or more advanced students could work individually or in pairs to make their own chart detailing other information about the planning or construction of the capitol and noteworthy past events. Encourage students to illustrate their charts.

Historical Events

What Do Students Know?

Explain that history is made all the time and that a historical event is something important that happened, either in today's times or in the past. Find out what students already know about a historical event that you choose to study by asking questions such as the following:

- Have you ever heard about [the event]? What do you know about it?
- Do you know where [the event] took place? When?
- Can you name some people who may have been present at [the event]?
- Do you know why people consider [the event] important? Explain your ideas.

Cross-Curricular Activities

Language Arts

Writing Captions *Explain that pictures can often tell stories. Help students gain an understanding of the event by showing them pictures that appear in either an art or picture book or in photographs. As you show the pictures, challenge students to suggest captions for them. Explain that captions tell what is happening in the pictures.

Writing Headlines and Topic Sentences **Use the art book or photographs to show students pictures of the event, and then challenge them to write captions, headlines, and topic sentences for pictures. Explain that captions, headlines, and topic sentences help people understand the main idea of what they see or read.

Understanding Primary and Secondary Sources ***Have students use the art book or photographs to write short descriptions of what is happening in the pictures. To contrast primary and secondary sources, have half the class write first-person accounts from the perspectives of people who lived through the event, and the other half write third-person accounts to explain what happened.

Levels of Difficulty

*Easiest, for younger or struggling students and for young English Language Learners (ELLs) and newcomers

**Average difficulty, for older on-grade-level students or more-advanced younger students and for transitioning or mainstreamed English Language Learners (ELLs)

***Most challenging, for above-average, advanced, and gifted students

Social Studies/Government

Planning Historical Events Explain to students that lawmakers and other decision-makers plan events people can attend today to help them remember events that happened long ago. For example, a mayor or governor might decide to hold a festival each year to help people remember events that were important in the history of the city or state.

*As a class, brainstorm events you might plan to help people remember the event you studied, such as book or photo exhibits, festivals, fairs, parades, and poetry readings. Put these ideas into a chart on the board.

**Divide students into groups. Have each group plan one event that would help people understand or celebrate the event you studied. Have them answer the following questions: Who will be involved in the event? What will the event be? When and where will it be held? How will the event be organized or celebrated?

***Invite students to create a month-long calendar of events that would help people understand or celebrate the event. Their calendars might list events that could take place at a specific place, such as a public park or a museum. Help students find sample calendars by conducting an Internet search using the keywords "calendar," "events," and "state history."

Drama, Movement, and Music

Performing Skits Before class, prepare some short scenarios for students to act out that will help them form opinions about the event and why it was important. Have younger, ELL, or struggling students respond to simple questions about the event, such as "Pretend you have been elected president during the Civil War and you want to tell the people how you feel about slavery." Have a bag of simple props students can use while performing their skits, such as hats, aprons, fake beards, and so forth.

State to State

Appreciating Different Perspectives Have students choose other books from the *Discover America* collection to find out how the same event is presented in different states. For example, they might look for information about the Civil War in a variety of states. Have them compare the pages and discuss how different states might have very different ideas about some events.

Doing Research Projects

Preparing Museum Exhibits Plan an exhibit in your classroom that helps explain the event you studied and that might appear in a state historical museum. Have each younger student bring one item for the exhibit and explain its significance. For older or more advanced students, consider choosing three or four important ideas about the event, and assign each idea to a group of students. Then have each group collect items or create models that explain their idea. Have the students write exhibit labels to accompany the items they display.

Sequencing Events and Creating Timelines Help students gain an understanding of the time period in which the event occurred.

*Display a list in random order of sentences that tell what happened in a particular event. Ask students to arrange, or tell you how to arrange, the sentences in the order in which they occurred. For example, if you are studying the Revolutionary War, you might mix up and then have students order the following: The British colonists settled in America; England made laws that the colonists did not like; The colonists wanted to make their own laws; The colonists went to war with England. Create a simple timeline using the sequence.

**Provide students with books about the event and have them find additional ideas to include in the timeline. Help them put those ideas in the correct order and add them to the timeline on the board or create a new timeline on chart paper.

***Have students name ideas from the book and other sources that tell what was happening in the state, country, or world during the time the event occurred. Then divide students into groups and have them create triple timelines to show what was happening in science, politics, and culture. Have them combine their information into one timeline with three or more strands. Post the timeline.

Levels of Difficulty

*Easiest, for younger or struggling students and for young English Language Learners (ELLs) and newcomers

**Average difficulty, for older on-grade-level students or more-advanced younger students and for transitioning or mainstreamed English Language Learners (ELLs)

***Most challenging, for above-average, advanced, and gifted students

State to State

Recognizing Similar Events Have students work in small groups to search other titles in the *Discover America* series for an event that happened in another state that is similar to the event they studied. Ask them to explain how it is similar. Was it the same kind of event, such as a war? Did it involve the same groups of people, such as Native Americans, the Spanish, or the British?

Comparing Past and Present Events Divide students into groups. Have each group find a modern event in one of the *Discover America* books that is in some way similar to the event they studied. Have them discuss how the events are similar. Next, have them explain how time changed or could change the circumstances and perhaps the outcome of similar events taking place in different periods of history. For example, how has technology changed the way wars are fought?

Special Topic: Historical Events

Thinking Critically

Invite students to think about the event you have studied, and then ask the following questions to guide a class discussion.

- What do you think is most important about [the event]? Why is that most important?
- Why would someone want to read about [the event]? Why is it important enough to be written about in history books?
- Did you think [the event] happened for a reason? What was that reason? Do you think it was a good reason, or not?
- What makes some events remain important long after they occur?
- Has anything happened recently or during your lifetime that you think will be recorded in history books and remembered for hundreds of years? Explain your answer.

Extending Knowledge

Reading Historical Biographies Read younger students, struggling students, or ELLs a short biography about someone who played an important role in the event. Encourage older or more advanced students to read biographies on their own. Consider having students give their opinions of the books they read by explaining to the class what they liked about the books and why.

Visiting State Historical Museums Arrange a field trip to a local museum that has historical exhibits about the event or period of time you studied. If a trip is not possible, try to take a virtual field trip online. If you do plan a trip, study the museum's event schedule ahead of time to see if you can watch a historical re-enactment or a video that explains the event while you are at the museum. When you return, ask students: What do your remember most about the trip? What new information did you learn? What else would you like to know about the event? How could you find out the information you want to know?

Historical Sites and Monuments

What Do Students Know?

Explain that a historical site is a place where something important happened. Explain also that what happened was probably important enough that you could read about it in history books. Find out what students already know about historical sites by asking the following questions:

- Have you ever visited a historical site, either in this state or in another state?
- Can you name some historical sites in [your state]? (houses, buildings, churches, battlefields, villages, government buildings, museums, monuments)
- What did you see there? (or) Do you know what kinds of things you might see there?
- Why do you think those places are important?

Cross-Curricular Activities

Social Studies/Geography

Mapmaking Show students maps that have historical places marked on them.

*Give students a blank state map and help them locate the sites of historical places. Have students mark sites with Xs and label them. It may be helpful to add major cities to the maps before you give them to students.

/*Enlarge a blank state map and display it in front of the class. On the board, with students, write a list of the different kinds of historical sites in the state and create a legend to identify them (for example, a triangle for churches, a circle for battlefields). Have students take turns adding historical sites to the map, as well as topographic features connected with the site, such as rivers and mountains. As an alternative, you may want to choose a map representing your state at a particular time in the past for students to work with as they locate historical sites.

Social Studies/Art

Explain that places often do not become important until many years after people lived there or events happened there. For example, the house where a president lived when he was a boy was probably not important until he became a famous man. Talk to students or read them a brief account of a person's life or an event that made one of your state's historical sites important.

Levels of Difficulty

*Easiest, for younger or struggling students and for young English Language Learners (ELLs) and newcomers

**Average difficulty, for older on-grade-level students or more-advanced younger students and for transitioning or mainstreamed English Language Learners (ELLs)

***Most challenging, for above-average, advanced, and gifted students

Designing Plaques Invite students to design plaques that might be placed at [the site] today. Ask them to draw pictures for their plaques and then to dictate or write a sentence or a paragraph that explains what happened at the site to make it important.

SOCIAL STUDIES/LANGUAGE ARTS

Creating Posters Show students pictures of how people looked during that time period, the kinds of clothes they wore, and the kinds of homes and furniture they had. Divide students into groups and assign each a topic, such as clothing, furniture, housing, etc. Then have them find images to create posters that show and explain life in past times.

*Have younger, struggling, or ELL students label the pictures and write several words that describe what the clothing, furniture, etc., looked like.

/*Have older or more advanced students write short descriptive paragraphs.

Creating Artifact Displays **/***Divide students into groups and have them create displays of items that might have been present at [the site] long ago, such as period clothing, tools, machinery, buildings, and so on. Students may paste photos or draw items on cardboard and cut them out, or create them out of clay. Explain that items such as these become artifacts when they are found years later, and that artifacts provide clues to how people lived long ago. Invite students to prepare a card describing an item or to prepare a brief description that a tour guide might give.

Doing Research Projects

Making Travel Brochures Explain that historical sites are important because they help people learn about the past but also because they bring tourists to the area. Be sure students understand that tourism is an industry that brings money into the state. Have students design travel brochures for a historical site in your state. Younger, struggling, and ELL students can draw pictures in their brochures and label the pictures. More advanced younger students and ELLs and older students can add small maps and short explanations of the site and its historical significance.

Discover America State by State Teacher's Guide

Preserving Historical Sites Tell students that historical sites often contain valuable items and that preservationists take care to protect these items and the sites themselves. Suggest that students conduct an Internet search to find articles arguing for and against "wreck diving," or the practice of scuba divers taking treasures from shipwreck sites. Then have them prepare and stage a class debate to voice their opinions about the topic.

Thinking Critically

Invite students to think about some of the places you discussed and what took place there to make them important. Then ask questions such as the following:

- Why are [names of places] important today? (or) Why would someone want to visit these places today?
- Do you think people should have to pay to visit a historical site or monument? Why or why not? How might the money be used?
- In what other ways do these sites help the state? (tourism is good for the state's economy; promote education, respect for heritage, and state pride)
- Whose house might become famous someday? Why would it become famous?
- What other places in [your town or state] might become historical sites? Why might these places become important in the future?

Levels of Difficulty

*Easiest, for younger or struggling students and for young English Language Learners (ELLs) and newcomers

**Average difficulty, for older on-grade-level students or more-advanced younger students and for transitioning or mainstreamed English Language Learners (ELLs)

***Most challenging, for above-average, advanced, and gifted students

---

State to State

Promoting Tourism Have students browse through books in the *Discover America* series and find important "firsts" that might have happened at specific places, such as the place where the first railroad was built or the first airplane flight took place. Have younger, struggling, or ELL students choose one of these places and explain to the class why people might visit it and what they might see there. Have older or more advanced students do more detailed presentations that serve as travel advertisements. Have them use persuasive reasoning to encourage tourism.

Categorizing Historical Sites Enlarge a blank U.S. map and display it for the class. Divide students into groups. Have each group choose several states or a region of the United States and browse through the books in the *Discover America* series. Then have them create lists of possible places that might have historical importance and categorize them by type of site, such as burial ground, military site, famous home, church, place where a Native American group lived or where a peace treaty was signed. Agree on a legend for the map and write it on the board. Then have each group add its sites to the map.

Special Topic: Historical Sites and Monuments

Extending Knowledge

Visiting Historical Sites Arrange a field trip to a historical site in your area. If a trip is not possible, see whether you can take a virtual trip online. Before you go, discuss with students what they might see at the site, and then divide them into groups and invite them to prepare lists of questions they want answered while they are there. Assign half of the groups to find—during the trip or afterwards—the answers to questions about life at the site long ago, and have the other half find the answers to questions about construction and preservation of the site today. After you return, invite students to share their answers with the class. You might have to help the groups prepare their questions and answers, and give extra help to younger, struggling, or ELL students.

Making a Time Capsule Explain that many places become historical sites when artifacts are found that show how people lived there long ago. Ask students to imagine that it is hundreds of years from now and that their school is no longer where it stands today. Invite students to create either a real or virtual time capsule that contains items that could someday become artifacts. Have them put items in their time capsule that represent their school and that would show people years from now the kinds of things that happened there.

Natural Attractions

What Do Students Know?

Explore what students know about the state's natural attractions. Define the words *natural* and *attraction*. Ask questions, allowing students to look through their books for examples.

- What kinds of places are "natural attractions"? (Create a chart or web on the board, including, for example, beaches, forests, canyons, mountains, rivers.)
- How are these places different from places that are built by people? (They are part of the land.)
- What natural attractions have you visited? What did you see there? What did you do there? (Include natural attractions such as a state or national park.)

Cross-Curricular Activities

SCIENCE

Defining Natural Attractions *Review the web or chart of natural attractions. Have each student find an ordinary natural form (such as a flower, a rock, a seashell, a piece of tree bark, a blade of grass) and bring it to class. Then have them explain to the class in what places listed on the board they might find the item. List these forms under the appropriate places and then add other forms you might find there.

Defining Habitats */**Have a selection of books available in the classroom about animal habitats. Complete the activity above, and then have students suggest different types of wildlife and plant life that might live in the places listed on the board. Create separate lists for animal and plant life under each attraction, and challenge students to explain why the animals might live in those areas or why certain plants grow there.

ART

Reflecting Nature in Art *Explain that natural attractions bring visitors to the state and that artists, photographers, and advertisers help promote these natural attractions by showing their beauty.

Show students art books or photographs of natural attractions in your state. Set up an area where students can paint, color, or draw their own pictures during your study of the state. Hang student pictures in the classroom and label the display "Our State's Natural Attractions."

Levels of Difficulty

*Easiest, for younger or struggling students and for young English Language Learners (ELLs) and newcomers

**Average difficulty, for older on-grade-level students or more-advanced younger students and for transitioning or mainstreamed English Language Learners (ELLs)

***Most challenging, for above-average, advanced, and gifted students

Designing Travel Brochures Have students design travel brochures promoting a natural attraction in your state. Encourage them to download Internet images or cut out pictures from magazines of things they might see there, and to write catchy phrases to capture the attention of visitors. *Help younger, struggling, or ELL students label their brochures. **/***Have older or more advanced students write descriptions of the attraction and/or include maps in their brochures.

Language Arts

Identifying and Describing Natural Attractions *Divide younger students into groups and have them brainstorm words that are associated with a certain type of natural attraction, such as a beach, a forest, or a river. Then have a volunteer from each group say the words out loud to the class and have the other groups guess the attraction that is being described.

/*For older students, play a version of Wheel of Fortune. If necessary, review a list of your state's natural attractions before playing. Call on a volunteer to go to the board and draw large empty boxes for each letter in the name of a natural attraction. (Check to be sure the attraction has the correct number of boxes and will be spelled correctly.) Have students take turns guessing letters until someone guesses the place. The one who guesses correctly puts up the next puzzle.

Writing Poetry On the board, write a four-line poem with the class about a natural attraction in your state, including one line about the wildlife, one line about the plant life, and two lines about the setting. Then have students make up similar four-line poems about a natural attraction they choose. *Help younger or struggling students and ELLs write their poems. **/***Older or more advanced students may write their poems on their own.

State to State

Comparing and Contrasting Natural Attractions Have students select other titles from the *Discover America* series, each student choosing another state or small groups choosing regions of the country very different from their own. Invite students to compare and contrast some of the natural attractions in other parts of the country with those in their state.

Mapping Natural Attractions */**Have students choose a state in the *Discover America* series. Supply them with an outline map of the state and invite them to look through the book to find the state's natural attractions. Have them use symbols to mark and label the natural attractions on the state map. Encourage them to share their findings and create a bulletin board display.

Discover America State by State Teacher's Guide

Social Studies/Safety and Services

Serving the Public Have students brainstorm a list of services the staff at a local attraction should provide to ensure the comfort and safety of tourists (for example, bathrooms, food, safety precautions, a first aid station, grounds maintenance). Lead the class in a discussion of the following questions: Why is it necessary to plan before opening an attraction to the public? What jobs are created when an attraction opens to the public?

Planning a Theme Restaurant Have students design a theme restaurant that caters to the visitors of a specific attraction. *Help younger or struggling students and ELLs plan a menu with food names related to and named for the attraction. **Have older or more advanced students create their menus using computers, if possible, and giving more elaborate theme-based descriptions of the food.

Ensuring Safety Have students brainstorm safety rules they should follow when visiting an outdoor area that may have wildlife, hiking trails, and open water. Then have them list rules for their personal safety, such as not wandering off alone, not speaking to strangers, and so on. Finally, have them make lists of safety rules and/or design posters that caution tourists to follow the rules.

Doing Research Projects

Reporting on Geology **/***Have students research how different landforms in the state's natural attractions develop. (For example, was the canyon carved by a river? Was the lake formed by glaciers?) Then have students write reports that include labeled diagrams to show how the attractions formed.

Graphing Tourism Preferences *Choose four or five different natural attractions that students have discussed. Set up a bar graph form on chart paper, labeled with the places you have chosen. Give each student a square of paper. Then ask them to place their paper under the place they would most like to visit.

**Allow older students to choose the list of attractions. Then have them indicate their choice by a show of hands, tally the responses, and graph the numbers. Ask volunteers why the natural attraction they would like to visit most appeals to them.

***Help students find annual totals of how many tourists have visited the natural attractions in your state over the last five to ten years. Then have them graph the numbers to see when certain attractions were most popular. Ask students to explain how these numbers might be used to raise funds for preservation.

Levels of Difficulty

*Easiest, for younger or struggling students and for young English Language Learners (ELLs) and newcomers

**Average difficulty, for older on-grade-level students or more-advanced younger students and for transitioning or mainstreamed English Language Learners (ELLs)

***Most challenging, for above-average, advanced, and gifted students

Thinking Critically

Invite students to think about the natural attractions you studied and then answer the following questions.

- Are natural attractions permanent? Why or why not? How can people harm them? What can people do to protect and preserve them?
- People often have strong feelings about nature. Its beauty makes many people feel creative. How does it make you feel? How do people express what they feel? How do you?
- What kinds of jobs are there at our natural attractions? What would someone need to know to work there? Would you like to work at a national park or other natural attraction? Why?

Extending Knowledge

Visiting Natural Attractions and Photographing Nature

Encourage students to visit and take photos of a local natural attraction. If possible, plan a field trip to the attraction. If not, encourage parents to take their students to a natural park, a nature preserve, or another relatively undeveloped area. Invite younger children to take along a class mascot when they visit the attraction and include the mascot in the photos. Have students bring a selection of the photos they take to class, glue them on a poster, and label them. Have older or more advanced students write short descriptions of their photos and add them to their posters.

Reading Independently Encourage students to follow up on any interest generated by this Natural Attractions lesson. They might be interested in broad fields such as geology or environmental studies, or in careers associated with natural attractions, such as park ranger, forest fire fighter, or park manager. *For younger, ELL, or struggling students, provide a selection of appropriate level fiction and nonfiction books, magazine articles, or Internet materials. **/***More advanced students could get books and information from your school or public library. You might also want to provide opportunities for students to share information.

State to State

Making Travel Plans ***Have students plan an imaginary or future visit to one of our nation's natural attractions. Help them go online to find information about travel, tours, accommodations, and things to do at the natural attraction. Have them create an itinerary of their trip, scheduling their activities over the course of one or two days.

Natural Resources

What Do Students Know?

Encourage students to share what they know about the state's natural resources. Define the words *natural* and *resource*. Ask questions such as the following. If assistance is needed, students may look at the book as they respond to your prompts. You may choose to create a chart or cluster as the students give their responses.

- Name some natural resources (coal, oil, natural gas, gemstones, oranges, trees, rivers). Which of these natural resources are found in our state?
- How do we use natural resources in our lives at home, at school, and in the community every day?
- How would your life be different without natural resources?

Cross-Curricular Activities

Language Arts

Creating a Poem Have students choose a page from the state book that shows people interacting with natural resources. Write a poem with the whole class about the interaction on the page. Use information on the page as inspiration.

Scrambling Letters to Make Words *Have students write the term *natural resources* on paper or index cards. Cut the words into individual letters. Encourage students to rearrange the letters to make new words, for example: *cat, tan, near, true*. List the new words and have students use them in sentences.

Making Word Associations **Have students fold a piece of paper into three columns. Head the columns: Air, Land, Water. Then brainstorm words that come to mind when thinking of the three resources. Examples for air could include *plane, balloon, breathe*. Have students choose one of the three resources and write a paragraph about it, using words from the column.

Levels of Difficulty

*Easiest, for younger or struggling students and for young English Language Learners (ELLs) and newcomers

**Average difficulty, for older on-grade-level students or more-advanced younger students and for transitioning or mainstreamed English Language Learners (ELLs)

***Most challenging, for above-average, advanced, and gifted students

State to State

Invite the class to browse through the *Discover America* series, pointing out examples of natural resources. Then have students enlist the help of a family member to find an example of a natural resource at home and bring it to class. They may bring a stone or a twig, or a souvenir from vacation (a sea shell, a miniature oil rig). Be sure they find out where the item came from. In class have them create a display with each natural resource sample labeled, indicating where it came from.

Special Topic: Natural Resources

SCIENCE

Identifying and Labeling *Provide students with science or coffee-table books or state calendars with photographs that include natural resources. Discuss the resources in the illustrations with students. Then invite them to make labels for the pictures. They may copy, trace, dictate, or write their labels.

Categorizing Resources **Invite students to make a chart as they page through the state book and point out natural resources in the illustrations. As students find an example of a resource, ask them to tell whether it belongs in the category of land, air, water, plants, or animals. Include geological formations (mountains, plains) as land. Include snow and rain in the water category. Analyze the chart by asking the following questions: Which resource has the most entries? Which image from the illustrations appears the most (for example, trees or rocks)? What does that tell you about your state?

Planning for the Future ***Divide students into small groups, and ask them to imagine what life will be like fifty years from now. Pick one natural resource that each group will have to live without and ask students to brainstorm alternatives or new ways of preserving it. For example, alternatives to gasoline in automobiles are electricity and natural gas.

SOCIAL STUDIES

Playing Natural Resources Charades Have volunteers dramatize activities associated with natural resources, for example, picking and eating fruit or mining for gold. Have the class guess the activity and tell to which natural resource it is related.

/*Relating Resources to Industry** Have students divide into three teams: air, land, and water. Have each team give a presentation on how its resource category affects the lives of people in the state regarding jobs and recreation.

/*Role-Playing** Have students work with partners to create mock interviews with natural resource "experts." Have partners choose a page from the state book that features a natural resource. Use the information on the page as the basis for the interview. Have one partner take the role of the interviewer and the other take the role of the expert. Ask volunteers to present their interviews to the class.

Discover America State by State Teacher's Guide

MATH

*Solving Story Problems Using natural forms specific to your state, pose math story problems to students. For example: There were three [trout] in the [Missouri River]. A [bear] caught one. How many fish are still swimming in the river?

/*Taking a Survey Have students design a survey with a specific number of questions. Then have each student survey five people to find out what others know about the state's natural resources. On the survey, include questions such as What is the largest body of water in the state? Name [two] minerals mined here, or What is our main agricultural crop? Have students compile the surveys and tally the results.

Doing Research Projects

Caring for Resources Have students research and report on what they do at home or what their community does to help save and protect natural resources. Reports may include examples of how the Reduce, Reuse, Recycle motto can be carried out.

Working with Natural Resources Invite a guest speaker or have students interview a family or community member who works in an industry related to natural resources. Find out what the person does and what education and training is necessary to do the job. Be sure students ask about the challenges and rewards of the job.

Thinking Critically

Encourage students to think about natural resources and connect their knowledge to other related topics. Consider some of the following questions:

- Do you think there is one resource that is more important than the others? Explain your answer.

Levels of Difficulty

*Easiest, for younger or struggling students and for young English Language Learners (ELLs) and newcomers

**Average difficulty, for older on-grade-level students or more-advanced younger students and for transitioning or mainstreamed English Language Learners (ELLs)

***Most challenging, for above-average, advanced, and gifted students

State to State

Comparing and Contrasting *Have students choose two titles from the *Discover America* series. Ask students to create a Venn diagram to compare the similarities and differences between the natural resources that are in both states. **/***Have one group of students choose other states from your region of the United States. Assign other groups of students to examine books from different regions of the country. When groups finish gathering information about the natural resources in their assigned region, have the class compare the natural resources of your state's region with other areas of the country. Are certain natural resources found in particular areas? What other observations can students make?

- Why is it important to protect our natural resources? What will happen if we don't?
- How does recycling help save our natural resources?
- Can you think of any artificial products that have been invented to replace natural resources? (plastic for rubber, wood, and other materials; nylon for silk)

Extending Knowledge

Adopting a Cause Have students brainstorm a list of local or state issues involving natural resources. Discuss the issues and the impact they could have on your community. Then invite students to help draft a class letter or write their own letters to the editor of the newspaper, giving their views on a local natural resource issue.

Collecting Natural Objects Encourage students to collect samples of rocks and water when they visit the city or state's forests, parks, and waterways. Enlarge the collections by including other natural findings such as leaves, shells, and feathers. Have students create a display and share their collections with the class.

/*Graphing Resources Have students keep a chart showing how changes in resource availability affect the prices of gas, home utilities, and food. Invite students to chart or graph the price of gas for their parents' cars for a month, the price of their groceries or utilities over a few months, or the cost of heating fuel over the course of a year. Some students may wish to use the Internet to investigate longer-term changes in supply and demand of natural resources, such as oil, and their effect on the economy. Suggest that students ask their parents and other adults how the periodic scarcity of fuel, cost increases, and other alternative fuel options have affected (or may affect) their driving or home-heating decisions in the future.

State to State

Creating Natural Resources Maps Invite students to use the *Discover America* series to locate natural resources throughout the United States. Have them create maps with symbols to show where natural resources are found. Remind them to make a legend and to label their maps. Display the maps and other work about natural resources.

Discover America State by State Teacher's Guide

People in History

What Do Students Know?

Find out what students already know about the featured person or group by asking questions such as the following:

- Who is/was [name of person]?
- When did [name of person] live?
- Where did [name of person] come from or live?
- Why is he/she famous? What did [name of person] do?
- What else do you know about this person?

Cross-Curricular Activities

Language Arts

Choosing a Rhyme *Read the alphabet verse to younger, ELL, or struggling students without reading the last rhyming word on the page. Encourage students to guess which word might rhyme and make sense as the final word in the verse.

Creating an Acrostic **Write the person's or group's name vertically on the board. Ask students to brainstorm sentences about the person (or group), each sentence beginning with a letter in the person's (or group's) name.

Performing a Role **/***Encourage volunteers to pretend to be the person and to say or act out something the person might have said or done.

Enacting a Scene ***Invite students to imagine a scene in the person's life. Encourage them to work in pairs or individually, write out the scene, and then act it out.

Levels of Difficulty

*Easiest, for younger or struggling students and for young English Language Learners (ELLs) and newcomers

**Average difficulty, for older on-grade-level students or more-advanced younger students and for transitioning or mainstreamed English Language Learners (ELLs)

***Most challenging, for above-average, advanced, and gifted students

---

State to State

Locating People on a Map */**Help students find pictures or photographs of famous people, for example, the presidents of the United States. Display a large map of the United States and have students place each person in his or her state, or use pieces of yarn and thumbtacks to connect each person's picture with the state. This activity may be done with other individuals or groups of people.

HISTORY AND ART: DRAWING

Listening to Draw *Without having students open their books, reread the alphabet verse to younger, ELL, or struggling students. Encourage them to draw a picture based on the rhyming text, aided by what they learned in class.

Drawing Related Objects **Invite students to draw pictures of items associated with the person or group (or pictures of items the person or group might have needed).

Learning Through Art Enlist the help of your school librarian to find art books with portraits of the featured person or events in which the person or group participated. Invite students to observe the art work and answer questions such as What can you tell about this person from the painting? What did the artist try to show? What can you observe about the time in which the person lived?

CONNECTING TO STUDENTS' LIVES

Interviewing Adults Encourage students to talk to their parents and other adults about the featured person or group. Have students ask questions about how the famous person or group changed people's lives or affected the present day. Invite volunteers to share what they learned with the group or class.

Writing a Letter to the Famous Person *Invite students to think about the way(s) in which the featured person or group has touched their own life and times. Have younger, ELL, or struggling students work together to write a letter to the person or to a member of the group. Students might dictate the letter while you write it on the chalkboard (and discuss it). They might want to thank the person as well as tell the person about his or her influence on their life.

/*Invite older or more advanced students to write their own letters. Encourage them to tell how their life has been influenced by the person and/or what they admire about him or her. Encourage them to compare and contrast their life and times with the life and times of the featured person.

Doing Research Projects

Making an Oral Presentation *Have younger, ELL, or struggling students talk to parents, relatives, teachers, librarians, and/or other adults to find out what they know about the featured person or group and/or to learn a few new facts. If possible, have students bring in related artifacts or visual materials. Invite them to "show and tell" or make an oral presentation.

Discover America State by State Teacher's Guide

Writing a Biography or a Report ******Have students find out more about the featured person or group by doing research and collecting data. Encourage them to use reference books, nonfiction books, magazines, the Internet, and so on. The biography or report could take the form of a poster or computer-generated presentation, a short paper, or an illustrated booklet.

Making a Timeline *******Have student make a timeline or a chart showing what was occurring at the time the person accomplished what he or she did. What was happening politically, culturally, nationally? What were the important issues of the time?

Thinking Critically

Invite students to reflect on the significance of the featured person or group. Encourage them to relate the lives and times of the people they studied to their own lives and the world today. Some of the following questions may be helpful.

- Do you think that [person's name] made an important contribution? Why or why not?
- Who are other people famous for the same thing or for something similar?
- What qualities does a person like [person's name] need to have?
- Who in the world today corresponds to [person's name]? Explain in what ways.
- What are some special features of [specific group of people]?
- Where are [specific group] located, and why are they there? (features of the location, etc.)

Levels of Difficulty

*Easiest, for younger or struggling students and for young English Language Learners (ELLs) and newcomers

**Average difficulty, for older on-grade-level students or more-advanced younger students and for transitioning or mainstreamed English Language Learners (ELLs)

***Most challenging, for above-average, advanced, and gifted students

State to State

Creating a Timeline ****/*****Divide students into groups and invite each group to review several titles of the *Discover America* series. Have students research a similar event in different states; for example, when statehood was achieved or the accomplishments of famous women in history. Invite them to create a vertical or a horizontal timeline to display the information.

Special Topic: People in History

Extending Knowledge

Reading Independently Have students individually locate a book about the featured person or member of a group. For younger, ELL, and struggling students, provide a selection of library books from which to choose. More competent readers should visit the library to find a book to read—preferably a biography or autobiography. Have students tell about their book in a book discussion group.

Visiting a Museum or a Historic Site Arrange to visit a place associated with the featured person or group. You might go to a presidential library, visit the home of a literary or political figure, take a trip to see an exhibit or a collection in a museum, library, or historical society, and so on. If possible, have a guide take students on a tour. Prepare students in advance to ask relevant questions and to jot down notes or to sketch anything that especially interests them. After the visit, invite students to discuss what they saw and learned, and to share their notes and sketches.

Creating a Festival Invite students to imagine that they are going to hold a festival in honor of the famous person or group. Where would they hold it? How would they decorate the location? What kind of music or dance would they have? What kinds of foods? What kinds of speeches or skits? Would they have hosts and hostesses dressed as people from the time period? What kinds of costumes would they wear? Encourage students to plan creatively and comprehensively. You might want to actually hold a small (or large) festival.

State to State

Comparing Famous People Invite students to compare a person or group from your state to a person or group of people from another state, or from several other states. *Have students act out a meeting of these people, deliver words they might have spoken, create a skit or conversation, or stage a mock debate. For simplicity, select people who lived at about the same time (early colonizers, Native Americans during the westward expansion, or Civil War figures).
**To make the activity more challenging, encourage students to choose people from different periods of time and discuss their lives and accomplishments in view of the time in which they lived.

Discover America State by State Teacher's Guide

Plant Life

What Do Students Know?

Find out what students know about the plant life of your state by asking questions such as the following. You might want to create a chart or a cluster as students respond to your prompts.

- What are some flowers (plants, trees) that grow in [state name]?
- Have you seen any of these? What have you seen, and where did you see it?
- Do you have a favorite flower or tree? Describe it and tell why you like it.
- What is a symbol? (Elicit that a symbol is something that stands for or represents another thing or idea; for example, on Valentine's Day roses are often given as symbols of love.)

Cross-Curricular Activities

Science

Conducting an Experiment Set up the following experiments at the beginning of your study of plant life in your state so students can observe the changes that take place over several days. **/***Older or more advanced students can write up these experiments, documenting their observations.

Making Food Provide a plant that has large leaves. Have students cut out two or three circular holes in small pieces of black construction paper, and have them carefully attach their paper with a paper clip to a plant leaf. Put the plant where it will get sunlight, and water it as you usually do. After two or three days, have students remove their papers. Discuss the colors of each leaf. Ask students what sunshine does for the plant (allows it to make food). Continue the experiment by having students notice what eventually happens to the parts of the leaves that were previously covered.

Getting Air Provide a plant with many leaves. Invite volunteers to carefully coat both sides of two or three leaves with a nonporous substance like petroleum jelly, and keep track of which leaves were coated. Have volunteers also coat only the top of two or three leaves and only the underside of two or three others, again keeping track of which leaves received which treatment. Put the plant where it will get sunlight, and water it as you usually do. Have students observe the plant and discuss what happens to each treated leaf.

Levels of Difficulty

*Easiest, for younger or struggling students and for young English Language Learners (ELLs) and newcomers

**Average difficulty, for older on-grade-level students or more-advanced younger students and for transitioning or mainstreamed English Language Learners (ELLs)

***Most challenging, for above-average, advanced, and gifted students

Language Arts

Writing a Class Poem Invite students to look with great care at the illustration of the flower, plant, or tree in their state alphabet book. Then encourage them to contribute a line to a class poem titled "The [Flower/Plant/Tree]." Have each student start his or her line with the words *I see*. Encourage students both to observe as closely as possible and also to think creatively and make comparisons to other objects and shapes. Write the poem on the chalkboard or, if you wish, on poster board that students can illustrate. Begin each new line with *I see*. Here is a sample poem about the state flower of Michigan:

> The Apple Blossom
>
> I see five white petals.
> I see a center of yellow dots.
> I see dark green leaves that look like birds.
> I see thin branches covered with flowers.
> I see a tree that is light and dark.

/***Some students may wish to make up other poems on their own. They may choose to play music in the background as they read their poems out loud.

Drama, Movement, and Music

Moving to Music Select a piece of music unfamiliar to students, such as Vivaldi's *Four Seasons*. Divide students into groups, and ask them to select a season. Play an excerpt from the season they select, and ask them to create a movement story (or a dance) showing how seasons and weather affect flowers, trees, and other plants.

State to State

Comparing and Contrasting Plant Life Have students individually or in small groups select other titles from the *Discover America* series, choosing regions of the country very different from their own. Have them compare and contrast some of the flowers, plants, and/or trees in other parts of the country with those in your state. Encourage them to discuss how the flora has adapted to its environment.

Geography and Climate

Considering Environment *Help students discuss the environment that the flower, plant, or tree requires, making connections with your state's geography and climate. Students might want to draw the featured flora, including some geographic features and an indication of the climate and growing season.

/*Encourage students to consider characteristics of the featured flora that allow it to grow in its environment. They might write a few sentences or a paragraph discussing this.

Doing Research Projects

Researching and Reporting on Flora *Provide appropriate materials for younger, ELL, or struggling students to trace, draw, or photocopy a plant and to label its parts. Depending on what type of plant is featured, students can label roots, bark, branches, leaves, stems, petals, flowers, seeds, buds, bulbs, and so on.

**Invite students to work individually or in pairs to research a particular aspect of a flower, plant, or tree. Using classroom science books, library materials, and/or the Internet, students might report on the function of a particular part of the plant, how the plant grows, how the plant gets its food, the kinds of animals or insects that visit the plant, what the plant provides for human beings, and so on. The report might take the form of a poster presentation, a short written paper, an illustrated booklet, or an oral presentation.

***Students may research plants that are in the ecosystem where they live. Challenge them to get information on the characteristics and relationships of their plants with other organisms in their environment.

Levels of Difficulty

*Easiest, for younger or struggling students and for young English Language Learners (ELLs) and newcomers

**Average difficulty, for older on-grade-level students or more-advanced younger students and for transitioning or mainstreamed English Language Learners (ELLs)

***Most challenging, for above-average, advanced, and gifted students

State to State

Comparing and Contrasting State Symbols Have students select titles from the *Discover America* series to compare and contrast one or more state symbols (flower, plant, tree) or all state flora. Invite students to work individually, in pairs, or in small groups to create an illustrated booklet of the state symbol(s) they have chosen. They might label each page with a state name, illustrate and write a sentence or two about one plant per page, and arrange their booklet alphabetically by state. If they have chosen more than one type of plant, they could illustrate all the plants of the state on one page. Alternatively, they could group their pages to feature one type of plant, such as evergreen trees, found in different states.

Special Topic: Plant Life

Thinking Critically

Invite students to discuss the featured flora. Some of the following questions might be helpful.

- If the featured item is a state symbol, was/is it a good choice for our state [flower/plant/tree]? Why or why not?
- If you had to choose another [flower/plant/tree] as a symbol of our state, which would it be? Why?
- How important are plants to humans? What do we get from plants? Name as many ways as you can that we use them.
- Have you ever heard of a problem resulting from bringing plants from one place to another? What happened or might happen? Why?

Extending Knowledge

Visiting a Greenhouse Plan for the class to visit a greenhouse, nursery, or conservatory. If possible, arrange for a horticulturalist or other knowledgeable person to be there to talk to the class about plants, noting which are native to your area and which are not. If possible, bring a digital camera to photograph the plants and the trip. Students could use the photographs in creating a book or a display afterwards.

Exploring Art and Creating a Still Life or Landscape Show students paintings and/or photography of flora native to your state. Discuss the characteristics of each painter's or photographer's style. Encourage students to compare and contrast the different renderings of the plant life. Provide art materials of different media and a display of silk flowers, imitation fruit, or other durable props for students to draw, paint, or sculpt in their free time. As an alternative, students interested in photography may begin a portfolio or computer album of photos that record plant life native to your area.

State to State

Identifying Plant Origins Have students investigate how at least one species of flora from two or more states originated in that location. Is the species native to the state, or was it introduced from a different location? If it was introduced, why was it planted and who was responsible for planting it?

Discover America State by State Teacher's Guide

Sports and Outdoor Activities

What Do Students Know?

Find out what students know about sports and outdoor activities, both in general and in your state. You might begin by asking questions such as the following:

- What sports can you name? How many have you played?
- What sports teams play in this city or in this state? (If students have ever watched local or professional sports, ask them to describe those events.)
- What outdoor activities can you think of? (boating, camping, biking, hiking, rock climbing, and so on)
- Where are some places to go for outdoor activities? (national forests, nature preserves, parks, recreation centers, rivers and lakes, and so on)

Cross-Curricular Activities

Language Arts

Sharing Vacation Experiences Invite students to bring in photographs and mementos from vacations or other times when they participated in outdoor sports and activities such as camping, canoeing, fishing, rafting, skiing, and so on. Encourage students to explain where they went, who went with them, and what they did. Suggest that they write a sentence or two, a paragraph, or a longer account about one of these experiences.

Math

Playing with Numbers Provide students with copies of sports pages from local newspapers. Invite them to look at different ways in which numbers are used on those pages. Some students will see that players have numbers on their uniforms, that numbers show the score in a game, and that numbers are used to show how well a player performs. *Have students draw a quick sketch of a sporting event, such as a basketball or football game, and include as many numbers as they can.

/*Challenge students to make a player prediction. Students should choose one player and find his or her statistics, such as average points scored, average yards gained, or batting average. Then have students determine how many games are left in the season. Based on the player's average to date, have students calculate how many points, yards, or hits the player will likely make by the end of the season. (Students might want to keep track during the season to see how close their predictions come to the player's actual statistics.)

Levels of Difficulty

*Easiest, for younger or struggling students and for young English Language Learners (ELLs) and newcomers

**Average difficulty, for older on-grade-level students or more-advanced younger students and for transitioning or mainstreamed English Language Learners (ELLs)

***Most challenging, for above-average, advanced, and gifted students

ART

Creating a Collage */**Provide students with magazines, and ask them to find and cut out images of outdoor activities that can be done in your state. As a class, make a collage called *Outdoors in Every Season*. Use poster board that you have divided into four equal sections labeled *Spring, Summer, Fall*, and *Winter*. Have students group their images according to season and arrange and paste the images in the correct section of the poster. Encourage students to discuss their own experiences and to tell about their favorite activity for each season of the year.

Making Sports Silhouettes ***Provide pairs of students with butcher paper, pencils, dark tempura paint, and brushes. You may also wish to provide balls, bats, helmets, or other equipment. Tape the butcher paper to the wall. Have one student strike a sports pose, such as running or swinging a bat, while standing next to the butcher paper. The student's partner traces around the first student's body so that an outline of the pose appears on the butcher paper. Then have partners switch places. When they have each posed and traced, have students fill in their own silhouette with dark tempura paint. When the paint dries, have them cut out the silhouettes. Display the silhouettes around the room.

State to State

Comparing Outdoor Activities Have students browse through other titles from the *Discover America* series to find outdoor activities in different states. Discuss how climate and geography affect outdoor recreation, and invite students to make a chart identifying states and outdoor activities different from those in your state.

Playing Sports Trivia Have each student choose another title from the *Discover America* series and locate one fact about a sport or sports figure. Students should write a question about the fact on one side of an index card and print the answer on the other side. Have students include the name of the state underneath the answer. Collect the cards and divide students into three or four teams. Take turns asking each team a question, making sure that you are covering the answer on the other side of the card. If the team answers correctly, award one point. If the team guesses the correct state, award a second point. Play until all of the questions have been answered correctly. The team with the most points wins.

Discover America State by State Teacher's Guide

SOCIAL STUDIES

Using Maps and Creating Brochures *Ask students how someone new to your state might learn about places to go outside to have fun. (Remind them that local maps often show outdoor recreation areas.) Show students a map of the state or region, and help them locate outdoor recreation areas such as lakes, nature trails, and parks.

/*Invite students to name their favorite outdoor spots in the region. Then have them each choose one and design a brochure that tells about the location and activities that can be done there. Guide students in making a simple tri-fold brochure out of a sheet of paper, or allow them to use a computer program to create the brochure. Encourage them to include answers to the following questions: Where is the place? What do you do when you get there? What do you need to bring with you? Invite volunteers to share their brochures and to talk about their favorite activities.

Doing Research Projects

Researching Sports and Leaders on the Field Have students page through their book and locate sports figures, types of sports, and sports facilities in the state.

*Invite students to choose a sport they find interesting. Provide on-level library books, encyclopedias, and other resources for them to gather information about the sport, including its history and rules. Invite students to give a short oral presentation in which they describe the sport and how it is played.

/*Encourage students to use textbooks, library resources, or the Internet to gather information for a *Leaders on the Field* report about a sports hero. Students should find out some biographical information and information about the sports figure's accomplishments. Encourage them to consider women athletes, sports figures from the Special Olympics, and people who have overcome obstacles, such as physical handicaps. Have students present their information in an oral presentation or as a mock sports report on a television show.

Levels of Difficulty

*Easiest, for younger or struggling students and for young English Language Learners (ELLs) and newcomers

**Average difficulty, for older on-grade-level students or more-advanced younger students and for transitioning or mainstreamed English Language Learners (ELLs)

***Most challenging, for above-average, advanced, and gifted students

State to State

Making a Recreation Map Have students divide up and look through the *Discover America* books, taking notes and/or marking a U.S. map with the names and locations of recreation areas and activities. Then invite the class to create a large map of the United States showing this information, illustrated with drawings and other art, such as mountains, sun symbols, and so on.

Special Topic: Sports and Outdoor Activities

Thinking Critically

Encourage students to think more deeply about sports and outdoor activities by considering questions such as the following:

- Why do people play sports?
- If you have a really strong interest in a sport, or know someone who does, why is that interest so strong?
- Why do you think our society honors sports figures above most other people? Do sports "stars" have an obligation to their fans? Explain.
- What problems can sometimes arise in connection with sports? Why do you think those problems arise?
- Are there enough outdoor activities available in your area? If not, why not? What else would you like to see?

Extending Knowledge

Visiting an Outdoor Recreation Area Arrange a trip to an outdoor recreation area such as a nature preserve or a hiking trail. If possible, have a guide take students on a tour. Prepare students in advance to ask the guide relevant questions. Encourage students to use a journal to record interesting things they see or learn. When you return to the classroom, invite volunteers to share excerpts from their journal.

Reading Independently Encourage students to read newspapers, books, and magazines about their favorite sport. Provide a variety of appropriate choices for younger, ELL, or struggling students. More advanced students can get materials from the school or public library. Students might share what they learned by making a fact sheet about their favorite sport.

Playing a Sport Once students have discussed the sports that are important in your state, provide them with appropriate equipment so that they can play one. Take students outside and play the sport for a short time. You may wish to get assistance from a physical education teacher or a local coach. Emphasize safety, team play, and fairness.

State Symbols

What Do Students Know?

Find out what students know about symbols, as well as your state's particular symbols, by asking questions such as the following:

- What is a symbol? (something that stands for or represents another thing or idea)
- What symbols do you know? What do they stand for? (A dove is a symbol of peace; a heart is a symbol of love.)
- What are some things you see so often in our state that they could be a state symbol?

Cross-Curricular Activities

Language Arts

Identifying State Symbols *Invite younger, ELL, or struggling students to help make a chart of three state symbols. Depending on the alphabet book for your state, you might choose the easiest categories, perhaps the state animal, the state bird, and the state flower. Have students page through the book, looking at the illustrations and calling out possible state symbols as you write their responses in the appropriate column. When they are finished, circle or star the actual state symbol for each category.

/*Invite older or more advanced students to page through or scan the text of the book and come up with their own state-symbol categories. (You might want to give examples of some possible categories.) They might come up with categories that are not listed in the book but that they could research and fill in later.

Interviewing Adults Encourage students to talk to their parents and other adults about one or more state symbols to find out a few interesting facts about them. Invite volunteers to share what they learned and to show any visual materials they may have.

Levels of Difficulty

*Easiest, for younger or struggling students and for young English Language Learners (ELLs) and newcomers

**Average difficulty, for older on-grade-level students or more-advanced younger students and for transitioning or mainstreamed English Language Learners (ELLs)

***Most challenging, for above-average, advanced, and gifted students

---

State to State

Comparing and Contrasting State Symbols Have students select other titles from the *Discover America* series. *Younger, ELL, or struggling students can look for the three categories they identified earlier and compare and contrast them with the symbols in their own state. **/***More advanced students can compare and contrast the different categories of state symbols they identified earlier. All students might make illustrated booklets to display their findings.

Social Studies

Considering Geography and Climate *Invite students to discuss the state symbol, as appropriate (animal, bird, insect, flower, tree, and so on), in relation to the state's geography and climate. **/***Encourage students to also consider the characteristics of each state symbol that make it particularly suited to live or grow in its particular environment.

Discussing the State Flag and State Motto Have students find the state flag in their book, or have them print out electronic copies from the Internet. Encourage students to describe the flag and to tell what the colors, objects, and/or design mean. Discuss your state motto if it is on the flag or if it appears elsewhere in the alphabet book. If it does not appear, you might want to look it up (or have students look it up) to discuss it.

Creating a Personal Symbol */**Ask students: If you could choose any symbol (anything at all) to represent yourself, what would you choose? Then ask: If you could pick the state [animal/bird/insect/flower/tree], what [animal/bird/insect/flower/tree] would you choose? Why? If they wish, have students draw (or paste from the Internet) and label the state symbol on one half of a sheet of paper. On the other half, have them draw and label their personal symbol.

State to State

Comparing and Contrasting Geography and Climate Have students select titles from the *Discover America* series, choosing regions of the country very different from their own. Encourage them to look for appropriate state symbols (animal, bird, insect, flower, tree, and so on) and to compare and contrast the geography and climate in which those animals and plants live and grow with the geography and climate in which your own state's animals and plants live and grow.

Comparing Flags Divide students into groups to locate the flags of all fifty states and the District of Columbia. Ask each group to present the flags it found and discuss the flags' backgrounds. Encourage students to make observations, noting similarities and differences. As an extension, give students an opportunity to examine some flags from other countries, noticing which carry a symbol and pondering why they have that particular symbol.

Discover America State by State Teacher's Guide

Doing Research Projects

Researching and Reporting on State Symbols *Invite younger, ELL, or struggling students to create a minibook titled *My State Symbol Book*. Have students draw (or find and paste) four state symbols, one on each of the four folded pages, and label each symbol.

**Invite older or more advanced students to work individually or in pairs to research a particular state symbol, using library materials and/or the Internet. The report might take the form of a poster presentation, a short paper, an illustrated booklet, or an oral report.

Thinking Critically

Invite students to reflect on the significance of the state symbol(s) by asking questions such as the following:

- Why did the [name of symbol] become our state [type of symbol]? What special qualities does it have?
- Do you think the [name of symbol] is the best possible choice for our state [type of symbol]? Why or why not?
- What other [animal/bird/gem/insect/flower/song/tree, etc.] might be a good choice for our state [type of symbol]? Why? What special qualities does it have?
- Can you find any connections among the state symbols? Why might those connections exist?

Levels of Difficulty

*Easiest, for younger or struggling students and for young English Language Learners (ELLs) and newcomers

**Average difficulty, for older on-grade-level students or more-advanced younger students and for transitioning or mainstreamed English Language Learners (ELLs)

***Most challenging, for above-average, advanced, and gifted students

---

State to State

Making and Playing a Quiz Game Have students page through other titles in the *Discover America* series, looking for state symbols. Have them draw the symbol on one side of an index card and write a corresponding label (Ladybug, Ohio's State Insect, for example) on the other side. After constructing the cards, students can play a quiz game in pairs or teams by selecting a card at random from a tray or box and answering the question correctly. Simplify the game for younger students by limiting the number or types of cards.

Finding Identical State Symbols Have students examine the *Discover America* books or use the cards they made for the quiz game to find states that have the same bird, animal, insect, and so on, as their state symbol. Students could make charts or record the information on the computer.

Special Topic: State Symbols

Extending Knowledge

Finding More State Symbols Invite small groups of students to brainstorm possible symbols that do not appear in your state alphabet book but that they either have seen in other state books or can imagine might be a state symbol. Provide books and information for younger, ELL, or struggling students. More competent readers can use the library or the Internet to find their information.

Developing Individual Interests Help individual students follow up on anything that has caught their interest: flags, flowers, gems, rocks, insects, state foods, state mottos, and state nicknames. Encourage students to start a collection to develop their interests.

State to State

Comparing and Contrasting State License Plates, Mottos, and Nicknames Have students compare and contrast several states' license plates, mottos, and/or nicknames. Students can use the Internet and other sources as well as titles from the *Discover America* series. You might use, or help students use, the Index in the back of this Teacher's Guide for mottos and nicknames (listed under State Symbols). Have students discuss the ways in which mottos and nicknames relate to the state. When researching license plates, students should note whether the state motto appears on the plate.

Comparing and Contrasting Less Common State Symbols You might want to check State Symbols in the Index at the back of this Teacher's Guide to direct students to titles in the *Discover America* series that discuss less common state symbols. Students might compare and contrast, for example, state beverages, butterflies, dances, dogs, fossils, reptiles, rocks, seals, and so on.

Discover America State by State Teacher's Guide

Technology and Inventions

What Do Students Know?

To find out what students know about inventions and how people use them, ask questions such as the following:

- What is an invention? (a tool or device that helps someone solve a problem)
- Can you name some inventions that help you do everyday things? (Prompt students to think about inventions used in communication or transportation; for example, television or the automobile.)
- Have you used any technology today? What did you use and how?

Cross-Curricular Activities

SCIENCE

Understanding Inventions Ask students to look through their books and find examples of inventions.

*Have students choose one invention and tell what it does. Encourage students to explain, demonstrate, or mime how to use the invention. They may also draw a picture that shows one or two ways to use the invention.

**Explain that people create new technologies and inventions to solve problems. Have students work individually or in pairs, select an invention, and determine what problem the inventor was trying to solve. Then invite volunteers to share their ideas with the class. Record on the board the inventions and the problems they solved.

***Challenge students to discuss different ways of solving a problem. Have them choose an invention, such as a microwave oven, identify the problem it solved (heating food), and discuss how the problem was solved in the past. Have them imagine what they would do if they could not use the invention and describe a new or different invention that might work. Encourage students to think creatively and allow them to discuss future technologies that could replace existing inventions.

Levels of Difficulty

*Easiest, for younger or struggling students and for young English Language Learners (ELLs) and newcomers

**Average difficulty, for older on-grade-level students or more-advanced younger students and for transitioning or mainstreamed English Language Learners (ELLs)

***Most challenging, for above-average, advanced, and gifted students

LANGUAGE ARTS

Finding Inventions and Technology in the News *Provide students with local newspapers and magazines and ask them to browse through the articles. Have students look for pictures or descriptions of inventions and technology in the news and ads, and then share what they found with the class.

Making Posters */**Have students make posters and label them *Technology in Our State*. Along the left side of the poster, write the name of your state in large letters. Then have students cut out pictures, words, or phrases that relate to science, technology, and inventions, and glue them on their posters. Challenge students to find things that begin with each letter in the name of your state. Encourage them to discuss how people use the different kinds of technology featured on the poster.

***Challenge students to choose one item from the poster and write a paragraph that describes how to use the technology. Remind students to include words such as *first, next*, and *last,* which help a reader understand how to follow the steps that the paragraph describes.

SOCIAL STUDIES

Using Technology on the Job *Ask students how different people in their community use technology to do their jobs. Guide students by providing a few examples, such as doctors use medicines, x-rays, and microscopes.

**Ask students to think of one kind of technology that businesses and industries use every day, such as a telephone. Ask what life would be like without the technology. Prompt them to think about how people survived in the past without the technology. Then have students talk about their ideas as a class or in small groups. Encourage them to discuss how technology helps people in a community work together.

***Provide students with a map that shows industries in your state. Challenge students to think about different kinds of technology that are used by the industries described on the map. Encourage students to use books, encyclopedias, or the Internet to get more information about certain industries, such as aerospace or petrochemical engineering. Students should discuss the technology each industry uses; for example, aerospace engineering uses computers, rockets, and fuel.

Discover America State by State Teacher's Guide

Doing Research Projects

Researching Inventions and Inventors Request that students look through their books and locate inventors or inventions from the state.

*Have students choose an invention that they find interesting. Then provide on-level library books, encyclopedias, and other resources for students to gather information about the invention. Have students illustrate and label the parts of the invention and display the drawings in the classroom.

**Encourage students to use textbooks, library resources, or the Internet to gather more information about a specific inventor. Students should find out some biographical information about the inventor and learn about one invention. Students should recognize that women and men from all groups in society have made important inventions. Have students present their information by pretending to be the inventor and giving a short, oral autobiography to the class.

***Ask gifted and advanced students to research one area of technology, such as communication, medicine, transportation, or food production. Ask them to include examples of inventions that have had an impact on that specific area of technology. Students could present their research in a mock TV special, newspaper article, or computer slide show.

Levels of Difficulty

*Easiest, for younger or struggling students and for young English Language Learners (ELLs) and newcomers

**Average difficulty, for older on-grade-level students or more-advanced younger students and for transitioning or mainstreamed English Language Learners (ELLs)

***Most challenging, for above-average, advanced, and gifted students

State to State

Making a Map of Inventions Have each student choose another title from the *Discover America* series and identify at least one invention or type of technology described in another state. Then have students take turns showing the invention, telling what it does, and giving other information of interest. Have them create an invention map on the bulletin board, using colored string to connect pictures of inventions and inventors to their states.

Searching for Reasons Invite students to work in small groups and browse through titles in the *Discover America* series. Have each group choose three inventions, each invented in a different state, preferably in different regions of the country. Have students discuss (and research if answers are not apparent) why each item or product might have been invented in that state. Does the reason have anything to do with geography, climate, research facilities in that state, opportunities in that state, etc.? Provide opportunities for groups to share what they learn.

Thinking Critically

Challenge students to think about technology and inventions that they use and then answer the following questions.

- What kinds of activities do technology and inventions help people do?
- What do you think is the most important thing ever invented and why?
- What would you like to invent that would make an activity or a chore that you do easier in some way?
- How are science and technology related? Give examples.
- How has new knowledge provided by technology changed our attitudes and beliefs? (Prompt students to consider medical technology and ethical issues, industrial technology and environmental concerns, for example.)

Extending Knowledge

Reading Independently Encourage students to read about new technology in a popular science magazine, a newspaper, or a book. Provide a selection of books and articles for younger or struggling students and ELLs to use in the classroom. Encourage older or more advanced students to get materials from the school or public library. Provide opportunities for them to share information.

Designing an Invention Have students think of a problem that they would like to solve and then design an invention to solve it. Ask students to draw and label their inventions, and provide a place to display them. Discuss any technological advances that might be needed to make their invention a reality.

Visiting a Laboratory Arrange a tour of a local science laboratory to show where scientists work, the kinds of tools they use, and the kinds of problems they solve. Before the tour, have students prepare questions to ask the scientists. After the tour, discuss what students learned. Then have them write thank-you notes to the scientists that include the most interesting thing they learned.

State to State

Locating Science Centers Explain to students that scientists share information and discoveries. Ask students to choose other titles from the *Discover America* series, and challenge them to find other science centers or places where scientists work. Then have students develop symbols and a key for these places and add them to a map of the United States. Have them explain what kinds of things the scientists study at each science center.

Discover America State by State Teacher's Guide

Transportation

What Do Students Know?

Find out what students know about transportation and your state's transportation system by asking questions such as the following. If students need help, have them flip through the book as they respond to your prompts. You may want to create a chart with columns labeled *Air Travel*, *Land Travel*, and *Water Travel*, and record students' responses in the appropriate categories.

- How do people get from place to place? (on bikes, boats, buses, planes, trains, and so on) Do you always go in a vehicle? Isn't walking a form of transportation, too?
- What are some examples of things (goods) that must be moved from place to place? (cattle, cars, food, lumber) What vehicles are used to move them? (barges, tractor trailers, trucks, freight trains)
- What other kinds of vehicles can you think of? (ambulance, catamaran, fire truck, garbage truck, kayak, motorcycle, ocean liner, sled, spaceship, taxicab)
- What do you think are the most popular kinds of transportation in our state?

Cross-Curricular Activities

Reading/Math

Reading Schedules Provide students with bus, ferry, plane, or train schedules, or display an Internet site that shows schedules.

*Help younger, ELL, or struggling students figure out how to read the schedule. Draw students' attention to bold type, color-coding, abbreviations, and symbols. Help them glean information appropriate to their reading level and answer questions such as How many buses go to ____? What time does the first/last bus leave? How long does the trip to ___ take?

**Have students plan a trip to another city, using one of the schedules. Discuss what they would need to know to make the trip. How would they get to the station or terminal? How long would it take to get there? Invite students to record their schedule information on an index card for both departure and return. Have them compare the price of a round trip with two one-way fares.

***Suggest students compare two or three modes of transportation for reaching the same destination, using the schedules you have provided. Have them consider the pros and cons of each type of transportation, and then tell which they would choose and why.

Levels of Difficulty

*Easiest, for younger or struggling students and for young English Language Learners (ELLs) and newcomers

**Average difficulty, for older on-grade-level students or more-advanced younger students and for transitioning or mainstreamed English Language Learners (ELLs)

***Most challenging, for above-average, advanced, and gifted students

Social Studies

Connecting History and Transportation */**Discuss how transportation has changed over time. Ask students how people traveled in the past. (on foot, by canoe, horse, horse-drawn carriage, sailing ship) How did people get goods from one place to another in the past? (by pack animal, boat, raft, sled, train)

***Challenge students to draw conclusions about how improvements in transportation have affected commerce as well as individual travel. (Have them consider the effects of refrigerated trains and trucks, overnight air shipment, supersonic planes, and so on.)

Using Maps Show students a map of their city, town, or state. Have them trace a route to a favorite destination, specifying what kind(s) of transportation they would take to reach it.

Thinking About Safety Have students think about safety related to one mode of transportation—for example, car safety. Ask what makes car travel safer (airbags, laws such as driving on the right, traffic signals, seatbelts). Divide students into groups to consider safety for other means of transportation.

Considering Transportation Problems Ask students what they know or have heard about transportation problems in your city or state. Create a list on the board (traffic jams, flooding, potholes, accidents, and so on). Have individuals or groups choose a problem. If they were in charge of transportation in your city, how would they solve that problem? Have each group present their solution and discuss it with the class.

Science

Considering Space Travel Help students discuss space travel. What steps have already been taken? What challenges need to be addressed? (pull of gravity, fuel consumption, energy needed to leave Earth's orbit) Invite them to present their idea of what space travel might be like in the future if it becomes common.

State to State

Comparing Vehicles and Transportation Systems Have students browse through other titles in the *Discover America* series to find anything related to vehicles or transportation systems. Students could work individually, in pairs, or in small groups to create a chart that compares and contrasts which vehicles or transportation systems are discussed for which states.

Designing a Car of the Future **/***Challenge students to design a car that can take them faster and farther than they ever dreamed. What features would they include? Invite them to draw the car with labels to point out special features. Some students may present scientific support for their ideas. Students might work in pairs or in small groups. Provide opportunities for groups to share their innovations and drawings with the rest of the class.

Doing Research Projects

Researching Transportation *Have younger, ELL, or struggling students choose one form of transportation (bus, car, ferry, plane, space rocket, ship, train). Provide on-level library books, encyclopedias, and other resources for students to locate information. Have students find or draw a picture of their chosen mode of transportation and tell what they learned about it.

**Ask older or more advanced students to choose a vehicle and research earlier versions of it. They could use library nonfiction or reference books or the Internet to find information and illustrations. Invite them to present their research on three sheets of paper, presented chronologically, each with a drawn or pasted illustration and a few sentences describing the vehicle at that time. If more appropriate, they could present an illustrated timeline showing development and improvement in the vehicle over time.

/*Ask advanced and gifted students to research the history of the development of a particular transportation system; for example, the transcontinental railroad system, the construction of a major highway system, the U.S. mail delivery system, the construction of a subway system, the construction of a canal or other waterway system. Encourage students to use textbooks, library resources, or the Internet for information. Invite them to present their research in an oral or written report or a poster presentation.

Thinking Critically

Invite students to think more critically about vehicles and transportation by responding to questions such as the following:

- What methods of transportation are not as popular today as they used to be? Why are they not as popular?
- How did our state's geography and climate affect transportation in the past? How do they affect it today?

Levels of Difficulty

*Easiest, for younger or struggling students and for young English Language Learners (ELLs) and newcomers

**Average difficulty, for older on-grade-level students or more-advanced younger students and for transitioning or mainstreamed English Language Learners (ELLs)

***Most challenging, for above-average, advanced, and gifted students

- Do you think our state needs more public transportation than it has? Why or why not?
- Which kinds of vehicles pollute the environment the most? the least?
- What changes in transportation do you predict for the future? How will they change daily life?

Extending Knowledge

Reading Independently Encourage students to select books about a form of transportation that interests them. Supply a variety of appropriate materials so that younger, ELL, and struggling students have many choices. More advanced students can get books from the school or public library. After students have finished reading, provide opportunities for them to share information.

Visiting a Transportation Museum or Site Arrange a trip to a transportation museum or another related site. If possible, have a guide take students on a tour, and prepare students beforehand to ask relevant questions. Also prepare photocopied questions for students to answer during the trip, and have them bring materials to sketch objects of special interest. After the visit, invite volunteers to share their responses to the questions and their sketches.

Tracking Personal Transportation *Have younger, ELL, or struggling students keep track of each time they use transportation during a week and what transportation they use.

/*Challenge students to track their family's weekly use of transportation and to calculate the cost of transportation for an average month and then for a year. Have them find out about and include the "hidden" costs of driving a car in their final total (for example, gas, car insurance, oil changes, parking fees, tolls).

State to State

Great Names in Transportation Divide students into groups and assign each several titles in the *Discover America* series. Invite them to find people famous for their contributions to transportation. Post blank chart paper for different means of transportation and have each group talk about the people they identified and paste pictures and labels of the people and inventions to the appropriate charts.

4. Index

Contents
Discover America State by State Series. 86
Index 87

This *Index* to the *Discover America State by State* series includes references found in the state alphabet books for the 50 states and the District of Columbia. Each state alphabet book is indicated by the standard two-letter state abbreviation (see page 86 for titles in the *Discover America State by State* series).

Boldface entries in the *Index* refer to items found on the illustrated pages with the rhyming verse or to items found in both the rhyming text and the expository text in the sidebar. Lightface entries refer to items found only in the sidebar text.

The copyright notice of this Teacher's Guide permits you to reproduce the *Index* for purposes of classroom use. You may wish to allow older and more advanced students to use the *Index* to research their *State to State* activities and projects.

Discover America State by State Series

AK	L is for Last Frontier: An Alaska Alphabet
AL	Y is for Yellowhammer: An Alabama Alphabet
AR	N is for Natural State: An Arkansas Alphabet
AZ	G is for Grand Canyon: An Arizona Alphabet
CA	G is for Golden: A California Alphabet
CO	C is for Centennial: A Colorado Alphabet
CT	N is for Nutmeg: A Connecticut Alphabet
DC	N is for our Nation's Capital: A Washington, DC Alphabet
DE	F is for First State: A Delaware Alphabet
FL	S is for Sunshine: A Florida Alphabet
GA	P is for Peach: A Georgia Alphabet
HI	A is for Aloha: A Hawaii Alphabet
IA	H is for Hawkeye: An Iowa Alphabet
ID	P is for Potato: An Idaho Alphabet
IL	L is for Lincoln: An Illinois Alphabet
IN	H is for Hoosier: An Indiana Alphabet
KS	S is for Sunflower: A Kansas Alphabet
KY	B is for Bluegrass: A Kentucky Alphabet
LA	P is for Pelican: A Louisiana Alphabet
MA	M is for Mayflower: A Massachusetts Alphabet
MD	B is for Blue Crab: A Maryland Alphabet
ME	L is for Lobster: A Maine Alphabet
MI	M is for Mitten: A Michigan Alphabet
MN	V is for Viking: A Minnesota Alphabet
MO	S is for Show Me: A Missouri Alphabet
MS	M is for Magnolia: A Mississippi Alphabet
MT	B is for Big Sky Country: A Montana Alphabet
NC	T is for Tar Heel: A North Carolina Alphabet
ND	P is for Peace Garden: A North Dakota Alphabet
NE	C is for Cornhusker: A Nebraska Alphabet
NH	G is for Granite: A New Hampshire Alphabet
NJ	G is for Garden State: A New Jersey Alphabet
NM	E is for Enchantment: A New Mexico Alphabet
NV	S is for Silver: A Nevada Alphabet
NY	E is for Empire: A New York State Alphabet
OH	B is for Buckeye: An Ohio Alphabet
OK	S is for Sooner: An Oklahoma Alphabet
OR	B is for Beaver: An Oregon Alphabet
PA	K is for Keystone: A Pennsylvania Alphabet
RI	R is for Rhode Island Red: A Rhode Island Alphabet
SC	P is for Palmetto: A South Carolina Alphabet
SD	M is for Mount Rushmore: A South Dakota Alphabet
TN	V is for Volunteer: A Tennessee Alphabet
TX	L is for Lone Star: A Texas Alphabet
UT	A is for Arches: A Utah Alphabet
VA	O is for Old Dominion: A Virginia Alphabet
VT	M is for Maple Syrup: A Vermont Alphabet
WA	E is for Evergreen: A Washington Alphabet
WI	B is for Badger: A Wisconsin Alphabet
WV	M is for Mountain State: A West Virginia Alphabet
WY	C is for Cowboy: A Wyoming Alphabet

© Sleeping Bear Press. All rights reserved.

Index

A

agriculture, **AL–l, IL–d, IL–y, KS–c,** MO–y, **MS–a,** ND–a, NE–c, NE–g, NV–g, TX–w

crops, **AK–v,** AL–e, AR–n, **AR–s, AZ–y, CA–v,** DE–p, **GA–v, HI–n,** IA–k, IA–y, **ID–i, ID–p, IN–y,** LA–d, LA–y, **MN–s, MN–y, NJ–c,** NJ–g, NY–m, OR–m, OR–w, **SC–k,** SD–c, **TX–v,** UT–d, UT–i, **WA–a, WA–y, WI–c, WI–y**

dairy farming, **OH–d, VT–d, WI–d**

Delta, **MS–d**

livestock, **AR–p, CA–z, FL–c, IA–l,** MO–v, ND–b, NM–v, **NY–o, SD–r, TX–c**

Native American, MO–n

airplanes. see industry; inventions; transportation

amusements. see entertainment

animals, **AK–z**

amphibians, AL–r, NH–l

antelopes, **WY–p**

aquariums, **FL–u,** KY–z, **MD–i,** NE–z, NM–q, WA–z

Arbuckle Wilderness, **OK–z**

as pets, SD–l

bears, **AK–b, CA–b,** MO–g, MO–o, **MT–u, NM–b, WV–b, WY–g**

birds, **AK–e, AK–l, AK–p, AR–m, AZ–q, AZ–w, CA–q, CO–l, CT–a, DC–w, DE–b, DE–r, FL–m, GA–b, HI–b, IA–e,** ID–m, **ID–w, IL–c, IL–g, IN–c, KS–q, KY–a, LA–e, LA–p, MA–d, ME–c, ME–g, MI–r, MN–l,** MO–b, **MO–d,** MO–i, **MS–w, MT–o,** MT–w, NC–d, NC–s, ND–e, ND–f, **ND–q,** ND–w, **NE–d, NE–y, NH–d, NH–e, NJ–x, NJ–y,** NM–w, **NV–b,** NV–p, NY–x, OH–c, OK–e, OR–k, **OR–y,** PA–d, **RI–r, SC–w,** SD–p, **TX–l, UT–g, VT–h, WA–w,** WI–h, **WI–r, WV–b, WY–l**

bison and buffalo, **KS–b,** MT–b, ND–b, ND–u, SD–k, **WY–v**

butterflies, **AL–b,** CA–g, **CO–i, DE–t, FL–z, GA–t,** ID–m, **IL–m, MS–s,** OR–y, **SC–e, TN–z, TX–m,** VA–i, WV–b

cattle, **IL–o, ND–a, SD–r, TX–c**

cave, AR–b, **KY–m, MO–u,** NC–u, **TN–x**

cryptids, WA–b

deer, **AK–m,** FL–k, **ME–m, MI–w, NH–d, PA–d**

desert, AZ–d, **AZ–q,** AZ–s, AZ–w, NV–a, **NV–r, NV–z**

dinosaurs, **CT–d, MT–d, NJ–r, SD–t, UT–u, UT–v, WY–t** (see also animals, prehistoric)

dogs, AK–i, MD–c, **MT–s, NC–p,** PA–d, VA–d, **WI–a**

elk, WA–r

endangered, FL–n, **ID–w, IL–r,** LA–a, **NC–g,** ND–f, **WY–e** (see also concepts, conservation)

famous, **PA–p**

fish, **AK–h, AK–k,** CA–g, FL–d, FL–l, **FL–q,** HI–f, ID–l, IL–b, **MA–c, ME–h,** MI–b, **MN–w,** MO–r, **MS–c, MT–c, ND–n,** NE–y, NV–p, OR–c, PA–d, RI–v, **VT–f,** WA–f, **WI–m,** WV–b

horses and ponies, **ID–a, KY–e, KY–h, ND–n, NE–h, NJ–j, OR–k, SC–h, VT–a, WA–h, WY–h**

horses and ponies, wild, MD–e, **NV–j, VA–i,** WY–h

insects, AK–f, AL–b, **AL–e, AR–i, CO–i, CT–p,** DE–t, **FL–z, GA–h, GA–t,** ID–m, **IL–m, KY–v,** MO–h, **MS–s, NC–h, NE–y,** NJ–g, **NM–w, NY–l, OH–l,** OR–y, PA–d, **SC–e,** SD–p, **TN–h, TN–z, TX–m,** UT–b, VA–i, **WV–b**

Discover America State by State Teacher's Guide

mammals, **AZ–r**, NC–a, **ND–g**, NE–y, OH–n, **TX–k**, **TX–n**, UT–e

marsupials, **TN–o**

mules, **MO–m**

musk oxen, **AK–q**

National Wildlife Refuges, GA–o, MT–b, **SC–n**

prehistoric, **MO–k**, ND–l, NE–i, NV–i, SD–t, UT–u, UT–v (*see also* animals, dinosaurs)

reptiles, **AL–r**, FL–a, HI–g, **LA–a**, MI–p, NC–e, **NJ–r**, NV–r, SC–l

rodents, LA–n, MT–z, OR–b

sheep, **CO–j**, ID–y, SD–r

snakes, **AZ–r**, IL–e

water, CA–k, CT–o, DE–h, FL–d, FL–u, **FL–x**, GA–r, **HI–m**, HI–t, IL–r, LA–c, LA–o, **MD–b**, MD–c, ME–h, **ME–l**, **ME–s**, **MS–b**, MT–o, NJ–o, OR–l, RI–n, RI–q, TX–l (*see also* animals, fish; animals, whales)

whales, AK–o, CA–o, CT–s, GA–r, HI–m, ME–w, OR–p

wild, **TN–r**

wolverine, MI–w

wolves, AK–w, MT–w

zoos, CO–z, **DC–z**, **IL–z**, KY–z, MD–z, MI–z, MO–i, **NE–z**, OH–z, OR–z, PA–z, SC–z, TX–z, WI–z

artifacts, HI–p, **IL–a**, MO–k, ND–v, **NJ–a**, NM–a, **NM–k**, OH–f, OR–n, **UT–n**, WI–h, WV–d

Liberty Bell, **PA–l**

arts, AK–a, **AL–g**, **IA–a**, OH–k, **SC–s**, SD–c. *see also* people, artists

basketry, **NV–d**, SC–b

Harlem Renaissance, NY–z

jewelry-making, NM–j

Native American, **AZ–h**, AZ–n, **GA–e**, NM–d, NM–j, NV–d, SD–a

petroglyphs, HI–p, **NM–k**

pottery, **NC–n**, NM–d, **SC–o**

quilting, **AL–q**, HI–q, KY–q, **MN–q**, **NE–q**, **PA–a**, **TN–q**, **WV–q**

astronomy. *see* science

athletes. *see* people, sports figures

automobiles. *see* industry; inventions; transportation

B

beaches. *see* geography

bicycling. *see* recreation

boats. *see* industry, canoes; industry, ship building; military, ships; military, submarines; transportation, boats; transportation, ships

books, CA–j, **CT–t**, **CT–u**, DE–p, **FL–y**, GA–z, IA–f, MA–d, NV–x, **OK–d**

cookbooks, **CT–r**

dictionaries, CT–z

Brown Mountain Lights. *see* natural phenomena

C

canyons. *see* geography

capitals. *see* cities and towns

cars. *see* industry, automobile; inventions, automobiles; transportation, automobiles

caves. *see* geography

cheese. *see* food

cities and towns, AL–e, AL–u, AR–y, AZ–j,
AZ–o, AZ–t, AZ–y, CA–h, CO–a, CO–l, CO–o,
CO–t, **CO–v, CT–v, DE–w, FL–s, GA–s, IA–x,**
IA–z, ID–c, **ID–k, IL–a, IL–c,** IL–h, IL–i, **IL–o,**
IN–k, IN–v, IN–z, KS–c, **KS–d, KS–h, KS–k,**
KS–v, **KS–x,** KS–z, **KY–o, KY–q, MA–g,**
MA–s, MA–z, MD–e, **ME–y, MI–d, MN–x,**
MO–v, **MS–v, MS–x, MT–a, MT–e, MT–m,**
MT–v, NC–f, NC–q, ND–b, **ND–f, ND–j,**
ND–m, ND–o, ND–r, **ND–z, NE–o,** NE–u, **NH–s,**
NJ–b, NJ–w, **NM–q, NV–l, NV–y, OH–m,**
OH–w, **OH–x,** OH–z, **OK–e, OK–g, OK–h,**
OK–q, OK–t, OK–u, OK–y, OR–j, OR–o, **OR–r,**
OR–v, PA–k, **PA–t, PA–x, RI–f,** RI–m, SC–r,
SD–c, SD–d, SD–l, SD–q, SD–v, **TN–n,** TX–b,
TX–e, TX–h, TX–s, TX–u, UT–o, UT–s, **UT–v,**
VA–f, VA–w, WA–s, WA–t, WV–h

capital, national, DC–n

capitals, **AK–j, AL–m, AR–l, AZ–v, CA–s,**
CO–q, CT–h, DC–c, **DC–g, DE–d, FL–t,**
GA–a, HI–c, HI–o, **HI–y, IA–d, ID–b,**
IL–s, IN–i, KS–t, KY–f, MA–b, MD–a,
ME–a, MI–l, MN–t, MO–j, MS–j,
MT–h, NC–r, ND–c, NE–l, NH–c, NJ–t,
NM–s, NV–c, OH–c, OH–s, **OR–s, PA–h,**
RI–p, SC–c, SD–f, **TN–n, TX–a,** UT–s,
VA–c, VT–c, WA–o, WI–m, WV–c

center of North America, ND–g

villages, **VT–v**

civil rights. see concepts

Civil War. see wars

clothing, AK–a, **AK–q, CA–l,** CT–w, LA–a,
NY–z, OR–b

neckties, **AZ–b**

shoes, **OR–n**

coins, CO–u, ND–s, NJ–z, **NV–q**. see also money

colleges and universities, **AL–t, AZ–u,**
CO–u, IA–u, KS–n, **KS–r, LA–x, MA–h,**
MD–n, ME–u, MO–c, NE–r, NJ–u, **NV–u,**
OH–k, OK–f, OR–o, OR–s, OR–x, RI–p, TN–j,
VA–b, VA–e, **VA–u, WI–u, WV–u**

communications

computers, **WA–m**

dog-sled, AK–i

hula, **HI–d**

mail service, **CO–p, MA–z, MO–x,** ND–w,
NE–h, TX–e, **UT–p**

newspapers, **IN–v, NH–n**

pens, **NH–q**

radio, **WI–u**

satellites, NJ–i

telegraph, MO–x, NE–h, **NJ–i,** NV–g, UT–p

telephone, **MT–a**

television, **CA–t**

typewriter, **WI–t**

computers. see communications; technology

concepts

civil rights, AL–m, **AL–p,** AL–q, AR–e, DC–d

conservation, KS–u, MN–y, MT–c, NC–e,
ND–t, NJ–o, NJ–p, OH–n, RI–n, SC–z,
UT–x, WI–j (see also animals, endangered)

freedom, **DC–f, IL–k, KS–f,** PA–q, WV–v
independence, DE–d, NC–t, PA–i, RI–g,
TX–i, TX–s, VT–w (see also government,
Declaration of Independence)

peace, DC–t, MT–j, ND–p, **WA–p**

conservation. see concepts

Constitution. see government

criminals. see people, outlaws

D

dances, OH–k

Cajun, **LA–f**

clogging, **NC–w, TN–c**

hula, **HI–d**

Native American, **ND–d,** NE–p

square, **CO–s, ND–d**

Discover America State by State Teacher's Guide

Declaration of Independence. *see* government

desert. *see* geography

dinosaurs. *see* animals

disasters, natural
    American Red Cross, DC–a
    fires, **MT–i**
    floods, LA–u, **ND–r**
    hurricanes, **LA–h**
    tornadoes, **KS–t, OK–c, OK–w**
    tsunami, **HI–t**

Dixie, **AL–d, UT–d**

drinks, **RI–t**. *see also* state symbols, beverages
    juices, IN–k
    Kool-Aid™, **NE–k**
    soft drinks, **GA–w, MI–v, TX–d**
    tea, **CO–h**, MO–i, **SC–t**

dunes. *see* geography, sand dunes

E

earthquakes. *see* disasters, natural

education. *see* colleges and universities; people, teachers; schools

electricity. *see* science

Emancipation Proclamation, **VA–e**

entertainment. *see also* games and toys; music; people, actors and actresses; people, entertainers; people, musicians
    amusement parks, **FL–w, MD–g, VA–k**
    carousels, **MD–g, RI–c**
    circuses, **FL–r, WI–r**
    fairs (*see* events)
    movies, AR–o, GA–z, **IA–f**, IA–z, IN–b, **KS–y**, WY–d
    musicals, **OK–h**
    radio, **MN–k, TN–g**
    record players, **DE–v**
    roller coasters, **OH–r**
    television, **CA–f**, MS–k

EROS, SD–o

events
    Boston Tea Party, **MA–t**
    Chicago's World's Fair, **IL–f**
    Crazy Horse Volksmarch, SD–z
    festivals, AR–t, **AR–w**, CO–t, DC–n, DE–j, KY–o, LA–q, LA–y, MS–e, **MS–h**, ND–p, NM–f, NM–h, OK–i, WA–k, **WI–s**
    Fiesta Week, TX–s
    horse shows, KY–e
    Iditarod, **AK–i**
    Kentucky Derby, **KY–r**
    Louisiana Purchase, **LA–l**
    music, ND–p
    Olympics, TN–a, UT–w
    parades, OR–r
    Powwows, DE–n, IA–n, MT–n, ND–d, **NE–p**, WV–d
    Rendezvous, UT–j
    rodeos, AZ–o, CO–r, MO–v, **NE–b, OK–r, OR–c, TX–x, WY–c**
    rodeos, fishing, **LA–t**
    Salem Witch Trials, MA–s
    state fairs, **IA–i, KS–h, OR–s**
    Vandalia Gathering, **WV–v**
    World's Fairs, **IL–f**, MO–i, **TN–k**, WA–s

F

factories. *see* industry

fairs. *see* events

family history, UT–f

Famous Places, **CA–h, DE–e,** NC–x, OH–q, PA–l, **SD–c, WY–n**. *see also* Places to Visit

    Beale Street, **TN–b**

    boardwalks, **NJ–b**

    bookstores, OR–q

    Boys Town, **NE–o**

    bridges, **MA–u**

    buildings, **AL–o, AR–o, AR–v, DC–b, DC–h,** DC–p, **DE–o,** HI–a, **HI–i,** IL–c, LA–b, **LA–v, MA–f, MA–o,** ND–p, **NY–w, OR–t, PA–f, TX–s, UT–m, VA–p,** VT–q, WV–l, WY–k

    capitols, AZ–c, **CA–s,** CO–q, DC–c, DC–f, DE–d, **FL–t,** HI–c, **IA–d,** ID–b, **IL–s, KS–t,** KY–f, MD–a, MN–t, **MO–j, MS–j, MT–h,** MT–r, NC–r, **ND–c,** NE–l, NH–e, **NV–c,** OH–c, OK–o, OR–s, **PA–h,** SC–c, **TX–a,** VA–c, **WV–c**

    cemeteries, **DE–o,** VA–a

    Eastern Shore, **MD–e**

    Ellis Island, NY–i

    Family Research Center, **UT–f**

    gardens, **AL–b, DC–k, ND–p**

    Gateway Arch, **MO–a**

    Golden Gate, CA–g

    Great Lakes, **OH–e**

    homes of famous people, **AL–i, CA–x,** CO–q, DE–e, IN–l, **NC–v,** NE–a, NY–o, PA–j, RI–m, TN–e, VA–g, **VA–m**

    horse tracks, KY–r

    houses, MA–u

    landmarks, IA–a, **MD–i, MT–p, PA–l, WA–s**

    lighthouses, CA–a, **GA–i,** MA–x, **MD–l, ME–q,** MI–h, **NC–c,** NJ–s, NY–o, **RI–l**

    Lost Colony, **NC–l**

    mineral springs, **WV–w**

    missions, **AZ–x,** CA–e, **CA–m, NM–m**

    mounds, **GA–e,** IL–a, **MO–n, WI–e, WV–d**

    National Mall, **DC–n,** DC–v

    neighborhoods, CA–c, CA–w, **LA–v, RI–e, RI–f, SC–r**

    observatories, AZ–a, HI–h, ME–z, **WA–g,** WV–n

    Peace Arch, **WA–p**

    plantation houses, **LA–r, MS–l, SC–d**

    prisons, **CA–a**

    ranches, NY–o

    restaurants, **OK–e,** RI–d

    shipyards, **DC–y**

    space centers, **AL–x, FL–n,** TX–h

    statues, **AL–e, AL–v, DC–f, DC–i,** DE–p, GA–a, GA–s, **MA–d,** MN–t, NC–q, ND–b, NH–e, **NJ–l,** NJ–r, NY–i, OR–s, **RI–i, TX–a** (*see also* Places to Visit)

    stores, **MN–m, SD–w**

    train stations, **DC–u**

    waterfalls, **GA–m, MD–m, MI–t,** NC–a, **NY–n,** OR–g, **PA–f,** TN–l

    White House, **DC–h**

    White House lawn, **DC–e**

films. *see* industry, entertainment

fire fighting, GA–s, **IL–q**

flags, DC–f, DC–s. *see also* state symbols

floods. *see* disasters, natural

flowers. *see* plants

folklore, GA–z, WA–i

food, AK–h, AL–k, **AR–s, AR–w, KS–h, KS–p,** KS–v, **LA–b,** MA–b, **ME–b, ME–l, ME–n,** MS–c, **ND–k, NM–f, NM–r, OH–q, OK–k, PA–m, RI–r, RI–t, VT–i, VT–m**. *see also* agriculture; plants, berries; plants, fruits; plants, vegetables

    bake mixes, **MI–j**

    cactus, **AZ–s, ND–x**

    cereal, **MI–k**

    cheese, OH–d, OR–t, VT–d, WI–d

Discover America State by State Teacher's Guide

hunting, **AK–a,** AK–u

Jell-O™, **NY–j**

luaus, HI–l

potato chips, **NY–p**

seafood, MD–w (*see also* industry, seafood)

forests. *see* Places to Visit, national forests; Places to Visit, state parks; plants, trees

frontier, **OR–o**

Last Frontier, AK–l

G

games and toys, AZ–i, **GA–x,** MO–n, **MS–f, MS–t,** NJ–b, **RI–h**

gardens. *see* plants

gems. *see* natural resources; state symbols

geography, CO–p, **DE–m, DE–x,** MA–a, **MI–m, MS–x, NJ–h, NJ–p, OH–n,** TX–f, VA–n, **VT–k,** WI–n

basins, OR–k

bays, CA–g, **MD–c, RI–n**

beaches, **DE–j, FL–b,** MD–e, NJ–b, **NJ–s, SC–g,** VA–v

canyons, **AZ–g, OR–h**

caves, **AL–c, AR–b, IN–w, MO–u, NC–u, NM–c,** NV–n, **OR–l, PA–c, SD–j,** TN–l, **TN–x, VA–l, WV–l**

center of continental United States, **KS–x**

center of North America, ND–g

center of United States, **SD–x**

coastal plain, **VA–t**

Delta, **LA–d, MS–d**

desert, **AZ–d**

elevation, CO–a

Four Corners, **AZ–f, CO–f, UT–f**

gulfs, **LA–g**

harbors, **MI–h, MN–d**

islands, **CA–a, DC–i, DE–i, FL–k, GA–i, HI–o,** HI–x, **MA–i, ME–i, MI–i, NC–o, NH–i, OR–i, RI–b, SC–j, VA–i,** VA–t, **WA–i,** WI–a

lakes, **AZ–l, FL–l, KS–m,** LA–u, LA–w, **MA–u, MI–g, MN–l, MS–g, MT–f,** ND–r, NE–n, NH–j, **NV–p, OH–e, OK–e, OR–i,** OR–k, SC–n, **SD–g, UT–l, VT–l,** VT–u, **WI–l**

maps, MO–s

marshes, **WI–h**

mountains, **AK–d,** AR–h, CA–y, **CO–e,** CO–m, CO–o, **CO–r,** CO–z, **GA–m, GA–y,** HI–v, **ID–m,** MD–m, **ME–k, MO–o, NC–a, NC–g, NC–u,** NH–t, NV–n, **NY–a, OR–t,** OR–v, SC–u, **TN–a, TN–u, UT–w, VT–g, WA–r, WV–a, WV–m, WY–a, WY–b**

oceans, **CA–o,** FL–b, **ME–t, OR–p,** WA–p

panhandles, FL–t, **OK–p, WV–p**

pastures, HI–u

peninsulas, FL–b, MI–m, NJ–a, NJ–n, NJ–p

plains, ND–u, **NE–g,** OK–z

ports, **MS–p, NJ–n**

prairie, IL–b, **IL–p, KS–u, MN–y**

regions, **MN–b, SC–u**

river gorges, CO–r, **ID–d**

rivers, **AK–y, AL–a,** AL–w, CO–k, CO–y, CT–q, DC–p, DC–r, **FL–e,** GA–o, ID–d, ID–o, **ID–r,** IL–c, IL–r, IN–e, **IN–o,** LA–w, **MA–y, MN–i,** MN–r, MO–n, MO–q, **MO–r, MS–r, MS–y, MT–y,** NC–r, **NC–y, ND–r,** NE–d, **NE–n,** NM–q, NV–k, OR–w, **SC–d,** TN–a, **TX–r,** TX–s, VA–s, VA–t, **WA–c, WA–t,** WA–y, **WV–k, WV–r** (*see also* transportation)

sand dunes, **CO–d, IN–d, MI–s**

sounds, WA–i

springs, **AR–v,** CO–s, **MO–b**

springs, hot, **ID–h**
springs, mineral, **WV–w**
swamps, **GA–o**, SC–f, VA–t
time zones, **HI–z**, TX–f
tundra, **AK–t**, WY–a
valleys, **CA–d, CA–y,** OR–j, **OR–w,** VA–s, **WV–k**
wetlands, ND–q

geology
 earthquakes, **MO–q**
 fossils, AZ–g, **AZ–p,** CA–n, CO–f, **CT–d,** DE–h, ID–a, **IL–m,** IL–t, KS–q, **MS–z,** MT–d, ND–l, NE–i, NV–i, **NV–m, OR–f, UT–u, UT–v,** WA–c, WY–q, WY–t
 geysers, **WY–o**
 ice age, **NE–i**
 rock exposure, MD–s
 rocks, **GA–q, MA–r, ME–r,** MO–l, NC–a, **OH–f, OR–e, RI–v, VT–g**
 satellite observation, **SD–o**
 springs, hot, **ID–h**
 volcanoes, **HI–v, ID–c,** OR–i, **OR–v, WA–v**

Girl Scouts. *see* organizations
government, **KY–c.** *see also* people
Bill of Rights, DC–a
commonwealths, KY–u, VA–c
Congress, DC–f
Constitution, DC–a, **DE–f,** KY–x, NH–q, PA–i
 Declaration of Independence, DC–a, KY–x, NH–q, PA–i, **PA–l,** PA–v
 elections, **NH–p**
 Emancipation Proclamation, **VA–e**
 embassies, DC–k
 forms of, CT–f, **NE–l,** VT–c, **VT–t**
 Iroquois Confederacy, influences of, NY–d
 laws, making, **NY–m**
 political parties, **NH–r**

town halls, NH–v
town meetings, **VT–t**
vote, right to, **IA–c,** NH–p, **NY–s,** VT–c, **WY–f**
women's rights, **IA–c, NY–s, WY–f**

H

hiking. *see* recreation
holidays
 Arbor Day, **NE–a**
 Armed Forces Day, WA–u
 Chinese New Year, **CA–c**
 Christmas, **CO–n, DC–t,** DE–a
 Easter, **DC–e,** FL–j
 Father's Day, WA–f
 Fourth of July, CT–i
 Groundhog Day, PA–p
 King's Day, LA–k
 Mardi Gras, AL–u, **LA–m**
 Mother's Day, **WV–j**
 state, CA–v, HI–s
 Thanksgiving, **NH–h**
 Valentine's Day, CO–l
hospitals, **MD–x,** PA–m
houses, famous. *see* Famous Places, homes of famous people; Famous Places, houses
houses, types of
 log cabins, **DE–l**
 plantation, **LA–r, MS–l, SC–d**
 pueblo, **NM–p**
sod, **NE–s, SD–h**
hunting, **AK–a,** AK–u, ID–a, **NC–p,** PA–d, WY–v. *see also* industry, whaling
 hunters, **WY–z**

Discover America State by State Teacher's Guide

I

ice age. *see* geology

industry, **AL–v, ND–m,** OR–w, PA–o, **TX–d, WV–i,** WV–x
- airplane, KS–a, **KS–w,** MO–z, WA–b
- automobile, **IN–k,** MI–d
- bicycle, CO–s
- canoes, ME–o
- carpet, **GA–d**
- cattle, **KS–k**
- clothing, CA–l
- coal gasification, ND–z
- entertainment, CA–h, HI–i
- factories, **NH–m, NJ–f, PA–e**
- food, IA–k, **IA–q, MI–k,** ND–y, NJ–t, **OH–q, OK–y,** VT–i
- furniture, **MS–u**
- glass making, **WV–g**
- Industrial Revolution, CT–w, RI–j, RI–s
- jewelry, **RI–j**
- lumber, ME–f, **MN–f,** MO–w
- mining, **MN–u,** MO–l, WY–u
- music, MI–d
- playground equipment, MS–f
- quilting, AL–q
- restaurants, **KY–k**
- seafood, CT–o, MD–w, ME–h, **NJ–o**
- ship building, AL–u, ME–f, NC–t, OR–u
- shoes, athletic, **OR–n**
- soap, ND–m
- sports, **KY–l**
- steel, PA–o
- sugar, ND–f
- tourism, **FL–v, ME–v,** NJ–r, NM–t, WI–w, WY–b, WY–n
- whaling, CA–o, CT–s, MA–g, NJ–n

insects. *see* animals

institutions. *see* organizations

inventions, **CT–w, DE–g,** IN–k, IN–m, **MI–j, PA–i,** VA–w, VT–w. *see also* science
- airplanes, **NC–k, OH–w**
- artificial heart, **UT–k**
- automobiles, **IN–k, MI–q**
- basketball, IN–b
- cake pans, **MN–b**
- camera, Kodak™, ND–f, **NY–k**
- chewing gum, **OH–i**
- cotton gin, GA–s
- crayons, **PA–e**
- drinks, **GA–w,** IN–k, **MI–v,** MO–i, **NE–k, TX–d**
- Ferris Wheel, **IL–f**
- food, MO–i, **NY–j, NY–p**
- games, MA–b
- hard hats, NV–h
- home appliances, **IA–m, OH–v**
- light bulb, **NJ–e**
- lights, **OH–i**
- mills, yarn spinning, **RI–s**
- oil drills, PA–t
- radio, **WI–u**
- record players, **DE–v**
- restaurants, **RI–d**
- rockets, **AL–x**
- shoes, athletic, **OR–n**
- telegraph, **NJ–i**
- television, **CA–t,** ID–t
- tractors, **IA–t, IL–d**
- typewriter, **WI–t**

islands. *see* geography

J

jewelry, **NM–j, RI–j**

jewels. *see* natural resources, gems

K

kings. *see* people, royalty

L

lakes. *see* geography

landmarks. *see* Places to Visit

languages, NM–g, VA–t
    dictionaries, CT–z
    Hawaiian, **HI–a,** HI–w
    Native American, **MA–a, NH–j, OK–a, TN–s, WV–k**

legends, **WA–b**

leis, **HI–l**

libraries, **DC–l,** DE–e, **IL–h, IN–v,** NH–v

M

medicine. *see* hospitals; inventions, artificial heart; people, doctors; people, nurses

meteors and meteorites. *see* natural phenomena

military
    cemeteries, **VA–a**
    forts, AL–u, **DE–i, FL–s,** ID–o, **KS–f, KY–x, MD–f,** ND–u, **NY–t, OK–f, OR–a,** SC–j, SC–p, VT–e, **WY–x**
    Navy, DC–y, VA–f, **WA–u**
    Pentagon, **VA–p**
    service academies, **CO–u, MD–n**
    ships, **AL–u, AR–u,** IA–w, **ME–e,** NJ–j, OR–u, **PA–s, SD–u,** VA–f, **WA–u**
    submarines, **CT–g,** NJ–i, **SC–x**

mining. *see* industry; natural resources

money. *see also* coins
    United States Mint, CO–u, NV–q

mottos. *see* state symbols

mountains. *see* geography

movies. *see* entertainment; industry, entertainment

music, **DE–v,** HI–d, **ID–x, LA–z, MA–t,** MI–d, ND–p, **OK–m,** WY–c. *see also* songs
    Blues, MS–d, **TN–b**
    instruments, **HI–u,** KS–j, **MO–f, PA–l**
    jazz, **DC–j, IA–b, KS–j**
    Mormon Tabernacle Choir, **UT–m**
    musicals, **OK–h**
    national anthem, **MD–k**

N

national anthem, **DC–s, MD–k**

national symbols, NM–b
    march, DC–j
    song, **DC–s**
    Uncle Sam, **NH–u, NY–u**

natural phenomena
    Brown Mountain Lights, **NC–b**
    meteors and meteorites, **AL–n, AZ–m,** OR–e
    Northern Lights, **AK–n,** ME–z
    rainbows, HI–r

natural resources, AR–n, **HI–n, MI–o, NM–n,** OR–p, **VA–n,** WV–x
    coal, **PA–c, UT–c, WV–i, WY–u**
    copper, **AZ–c, AZ–j, MT–a, UT–c**

gems, **AR–d,** CO–a, FL–n, **GA–q,** ID–g, **LA–o, MN–a,** NC–a, NM–j, **OH–f,** TN–u, VT–g, WA–g

glaciers, **AK–g,** CA–y, IN–d, MA–r, MT–g, NJ–h, **OH–g,** SD–g, **WI–i**

gold, **AK–j, AK–x, AK–y,** AZ–j, **CA–e, CA–g, GA–q,** ID–g, **MT–v,** NC–q, **NM–g, NV–e, NV–v,** SD–l, SD–q, **WA–n,** WA–y

granite, **GA–q,** GA–y, ME–r, **VT–q**

iron ore, **MN–o, PA–o**

lead, **MO–l**

marble, **GA–q, VT–q**

minerals, **AR–q,** RI–v

natural gas, AL–u

oil, **OK–o, PA–t, TX–u**

quartz, NV–g

rocks, **IA–g**

salt, **WV–i**

silver, AZ–j, CO–a, ID–z, NV–g, **NV–v**

stone, IN–w, NY–q

talc, **GA–q**

trees, MS–u, **WV–i**

zinc, **ID–z, NJ–z**

newspapers. *see* communications

nicknames. *see* state symbols

Northern Lights. *see* natural phenomena

O

oceans. *see* geography

organizations

4-H, **IA–f**

American Red Cross, DC–a

Girl Scouts, GA–g, GA–s

Little League Baseball, **PA–w**

Seeing Eye, NJ–d

United Nations, **CA–u**

outlaws. *see* people

P

parks, CT–l, OR–r

pens. *see* communications

people, CA–x, **DE–p,** NE–o

abolitionists, CT–u, DC–l, DE–u, IN–u, KS–f, MA–j, NE–x, NH–r, OH–u, **WV–h**

activists, CA–v, OR–h, OR–i

actors and actresses, **IA–j, MN–j, MT–q**

African-Americans, **AL–p, AL–t, AR–e, DC–d,** DC–l, DC–m, DC–v, IL–h, **KS–l, MD–t, MO–p, MS–o, NH–b,** NJ–u, NY–z, **OH–k, OK–b, PA–b, SD–y, TN–j, VA–b,** WA–o, **WV–e,** WV–h

Amish, **IN–a, PA–a**

animal rights advocates, NV–j, SD–k

architects, CA–x, **PA–f, WI–f,** WI–q

artists, **AL–g,** CA–w, DC–v, DE–p, **IA–a,** IA–i, **ID–e, KY–a, MA–n, MN–c,** MO–j, **MT–r,** NC–n, NH–b, NH–y, NM–d, **NM–o, NV–d, NY–q,** NY–z, **OK–d,** RI–i, **SD–a,** SD–c, SD–m, **SD–z,** VT–g, VT–s, **WI–g**

Asian-Americans, **CA–c**

astronauts, AZ–m, **DE–s, IN–g, KS–e, NH–a, OH–a, OK–l**

astronomers, MO–z

authors, **CA–j,** CA–z, **CT–t, CT–u,** CT–z, FL–y, **GA–z,** IA–f, IN–r, **KS–l, KS–p, KS–y,** MA–s, **MA–w, MN–x,** MO–f, **MO–p,** NC–f, NE–c, **NH–h,** NH–i, NV–y, OK–d, OK–h, OR–q, **SD–d,** WV–h, **WY–z**

Basque, **ID–x,** WY–s

businesspeople, DE–c, ID–p, IL–w, **KS–h,** KS–p, **KY–k,** ME–b, NC–v, **ND–m,** ND–r, NE–k, OR–n, PA–f, **PA–m,** PA–o, TX–d, WA–n

Cajun, LA–f

cartoonists, **MN–c, OK–d**

celebrities, CO–b, IL–w

child prodigies, **VT–z**

Civil War figures, DC–b, **GA–y, IL–u,** MO–c, OH–u, OH–x, VA–w, WV–h

conservationists, **WI–j**

cowboys, CA–z, **FL–c,** HI–u, **KS–d,** MO–v, **NM–c, NM–v, OK–c, TX–c,** WY–c

cowgirl, WY–c

disabled, **AL–i,** ND–j, **NJ–d,** NY–r

doctors, NE–p, OR–m

Dutch, NY–y

engineers, DC–g

entertainers, **CT–b, MN–k, MS–k, MS–o,** ND–k, **OK–r, PA–b,** SD–l, **WY–w**

explorers, AL–u, AR–l, **CA–e, CO–z, CT–e, FL–j, HI–p,** HI–x, **IA–x, ID–s, IN–e,** KS–n, **KY–d,** KY–w, **MN–v, MO–e,** MT–c, **MT–p,** NC–r, **ND–s, NE–e,** NH–t, **NM–g, NY–h, OK–c, OK–z,** OR–a, OR–y, **SD–e, SD–v, SD–y,** VA–q, VA–w, **VT–l**

fictional characters, NY–h, **OK–d, OR–q**

Finns, **DE–l**

First Ladies, **DC–m**

folk heroes, **NE–f, OH–j,** WA–i

French-Canadian, NH–m

German-Russians, ND–k

Germans, KS–v

governors, ID–l, **KY–i,** LA–p, **MN–h,** NH–p, OR–p, PA–g, SD–f, **VA–h,** WA–l, **WY–f**

Hawaiians, native, **HI–p**

Hispanic, CA–v, ID–q

humanitarians, **WA–m,** WA–o

hunters, **WY–z**

immigrants, KS–v, ME–p, ND–k, NJ–l, **NY–i,** OK–k, **SD–i**

inventors, **CA–t, CT–w, DE–g,** DE–v, **FL–i, GA–d,** GA–s, GA–w, **IA–m, IA–t,** ID–t, **IN–k, KS–b, MI–q,** MI–v, ND–f, NE–k, **NJ–e, NJ–i,** NV–v, NY–j, NY–k, NY–p, **OH–i, OH–v, OH–w,** OR–n, PA–e, **PA–i,** PA–t, **RI–s,** VA–m, VA–w, VT–w, WI–t, WI–u

Isleños, **LA–i**

Italians, OK–k

Japanese-Americans, UT–t

Jewish, ID–l

landscape architects, **CT–l**

law enforcement, AZ–t, **KS–d, KS–g,** SD–l, **TX–t**

lawyers, **CT–j,** CT–z

leaders, **AL–p, AL–t, CT–h, DC–d, DE–d,** HI–b, **HI–i,** HI–j, **HI–k, HI–q, IA–h, ID–l,** ID–n, **KY–d,** ND–n, **NV–w, NY–d, NY–s,** OH–x, **OK–a, OK–g, OK–v, OR–j, PA–q, RI–k, RI–w, TN–s,** TN–v, **TX–h, TX–o, TX–q, TX–s, UT–y,** VA–j, **WY–r**

legends, **CA–z**

lexicographers, CT–z

mayors, DC–m, IL–h, **IN–j, WA–l,** WI–s

military figures, **KS–i,** MT–l, OH–e, SD–f, SD–n, TN–v (*see also* people, Civil War figures; people, Revolutionary War figures)

miners, NV–v, **WI–b**

missionaries, **AZ–x,** CA–e, CA–m, WA–m, WA–y

mountaineers, WA–r

musicians, **AR–j, CT–i, DC–j, IA–b, KS–j,** MS–d, **MS–e,** ND–k, NY–l, NY–z, **OK–m, OK–y,** TN–b, **TN–e, TN–g, TN–j,** TX–j, **UT–m,** VA–w, **WA–x**

Native Americans, **AK–a,** AK–c, AK–q, **AZ–h, CA–i, IA–n, ID–n,** IL–a, IL–b, IN–k, **IN–n, KS–n,** KS–o, ND–d, **ND–v,** NE–e, NY–p, **OK–a, OK–c,** OK–f, **OK–g, OK–i,** OR–a, **PA–n,** SD–a, **UT–n, VA–r, WI–n, WV–d,** WY–d, **WY–m**

Abenaki, **NH–j, NH–k**

Aleut-Alutiq, AK–a

Algonquin, CT–q, **VT–n**

Anasazi, **AZ–e, CO–m, NM–a,** UT–n

Apache, **AZ–i**

Assiniboine, **MT–n**

Athabascans, AK–a
Bannock, **ID–n**
Blackfeet, **MT–n**
Cayuga, **NY–d**
Cherokee, **GA–c, OK–t, OK–v,** SC–u, TN–s, TN–t
Cheyenne, **MT–l, MT–n**
Chippewa, **MT–n**
Choptank, MD–e
Coeur d'Alene, **ID–n**
Comanche, **TX–q**
Cree, MT–n
Crow, MT–n
Dakota, **MN–e**
Fremont, **UT–n**
Gros Ventre, **MT–n**
Hawaiians, native, **HI–p**
Hohokam, **AZ–e**
Hopi, **AZ–k**
in Mississippi, **MS–i**
Inupiaqs-Eskimo, AK–a
Iroquois, **NY–d,** VT–n
Kalispel, **ID–n**
Kootenai, **ID–n,** MT–n
Lakota, ND–n
Lenape, **NJ–a,** NJ–n, NJ–o
Lenni-Lenape, **DE–n, PA–n**
Little Shell, MT–n
Massachuset, **MA–a**
Meskwaki, IA–n
Missippian, MO–n
Mogollan, **AZ–e**
Mohawk, **NY–d**
Nanticoke, **DE–n,** MD–e
Narragansetts, RI–k
Navajo, **AZ–n, UT–n**

Nez Perce, **ID–a,** ID–d, ID–g, **ID–n,** ID–s, **OR–j,** WA–h
Northwest Coast, AK–c, AK–s
Ojibwa, MI–n, **MN–e,** WI–n
Omaha, **NE–p**
Oneida, **NY–d**
Onondaga, **NY–d**
Ottawa, MI–n, WI–n
Paiutes, NV–w, NV–x, NV–y, **UT–n**
Palouse, WA–h
Passamaquoddies, **ME–o**
Pend d'Oreille, MT–n
Penobscots, **ME–o**
Ponca, **NE–p**
Potawatomi, MI–n, **WI–n**
Powhatan, **DC–p**
Pueblo, **NM–p,** NM–z
Quapaw, **AR–k,** OK–q
Quinault, **WA–q**
Salush, MT–n
Sauk, IA–h, IL–b, WI–n
Seneca, **NY–d**
Shawnee, OH–x
Shoshone, **ID–n, ID–s, ND–s,** NV–i, SD–e, **UT–n**
Sinagua, **AZ–e**
Sioux, **AR–a,** MT–l, MT–n, **NE–p,** SD–a, SD–q, **SD–s, SD–y, SD–z, WY–r**
Ute, **UT–n**
Wamponoags, MA–m, RI–k
Washoe, **NV–d**
Winnebago, **NE–p,** WI–n
Yupik-Eskimo, AK–a
naturalists, CA–y, CO–e, **KY–a**
navigators, **NJ–n**
nobility, MD–o, **ME–y**
nurses, **DC–a**

outlaws, AZ–t, CT–v, DE–p, **FL–p**, KS–d, **MA–i**, ME–x, NY–o, **OK–j, RI–x, SC–q, UT–o**, VA–v, **WY–b**

philanthropists, DC–x, WA–p

photographers, **KS–p**

pilots, DC–x, DC–y, **KS–e**, MN–c, MO–z, **NC–k**, OH–i, **OH–w, WV–y**

pioneers, AK–j, HI–n, ID–o, IN–k, IN–o, **KY–d**, KY–w, MO–a, **NC–y, NE–b**, NE–g, **NE–j**, NE–q, **NE–s, NV–k**, NY–y, **OK–s, OR–o, SD–d**, SD–h, **SD–i, TX–o**, TX–w, **UT–h, UT–j, WV–y**

pirates, CT–v, DE–p, **FL–p, MA–i, ME–x**, NY–o, **RI–x, SC–q**, VA–v

poets, **CO–o, DC–k**, IN–r, **MA–j, MA–p**, MA–z, **NH–f**

politicians, ID–m, ID–n, **IN–q, MT–j, NH–r, NH–w, NH–y**, WA–l

Polynesians, **HI–p**

preservationists, RI–e

presidents, AK–d, **AR–c**, DC–b, DC–d, **DC–g, DC–i**, DC–o, **DC–q**, DC–u, **GA–j, GA–u, IA–p, IL–l, IL–u, IN–l, KS–i**, KY–y, **LA–j, MA–k, MI–f, MO–p, NC–j, ND–t**, NE–e, NE–l, **NH–Y, NJ–j, NJ–w**, NY–c, NY–o, **NY–r, NY–v**, OH–c, **OH–p, PA–g, PA–j, SD–m**, TN–p, **TX–h, VA–g, VA–m, VA–w, VA–z, VT–p**

printers, NH–n

prospectors, AZ–t

religious groups, **DE–u, IN–a, KY–p**, MA–b, MA–m, ME–b, NJ–q, **PA–a, PA–q**, RI–w, **UT–y**

Revolutionary War figures, **CT–k**, IN–v, **MA–o**, MA–z, **NJ–m, NJ–w**, NY–t, PA–v, **SC–f, VT–e**

royalty, CT–x, HI–b, **HI–i, HI–j, HI–k, HI–q**, HI–y, **MD–q, NC–q**, NY–y, VA–o, **VA–q**

sailors, **NH–b**

scientists, AL–x, **DE–s**, IA–u, KS–c, MN–u, **MO–p**, NJ–i, NM–l, OR–d, OR–f, **OR–x**, WI–u

settlers, **DE–k**, MA–b, **MA–m, MD–d**, ME–p, **NC–l, VA–j, VA–r**, VA–v

sheepherders, **WY–s**

soldiers, **OK–b**

songwriters, DC–j, **DC–s, KY–s, MD–k**

sports figures, **AL–f, AL–h, AR–z**, ID–k, KS–b, **KS–o, KY–j, MD–u**, MD–y, **ND–h**, NJ–u, **OK–v, OK–y**, SD–l, **TN–w**, WA–r, WI–p, **WV–o**, WV–u

Supreme Court Justices, **DC–o**, NH–r, WA–j

surveyors, DE–m

Swedes, **DE–l, DE–o**

teachers, **AL–i, AL–t, CT–c**, IA–c, IA–f, ND–j, **SC–m, VA–b**, VA–e, WI–k, **WV–e**

voyageurs, **IN–o**

water masters, **AZ–z**, UT–i

watermen, **MD–w**

women, **AL–i, AL–p, AR–e**, CA–x, **CO–t, CT–c**, CT–r, **CT–u, DC–a**, DC–d, **DC–m, DC–o**, DC–p, **DE–s**, GA–d, GA–g, **HI–j**, IA–c, **ID–e**, ID–s, **ID–y, IL–j, KS–e**, KS–w, **MA–j, MA–p, MD–q, MD–t**, MO–f, **MS–o, MT–j**, MT–q, ND–i, **ND–j, ND–s**, NE–e, NE–p, **NH–a, NH–h**, NH–i, NH–p, **NJ–m**, NJ–u, NM–d, **NM–o, NV–d, NV–j**, NV–k, NV–q, NY–o, **NY–s**, OH–a, OK–q, **OK–v**, OR–o, RI–e, **RI–l**, RI–w, SC–i, **SC–m**, SD–e, **SD–l, TN–w, VA–q, VA–r**, VT–g, WA–l, WA–r, **WI–g, WV–e**, WV–h, WV–i, **WV–o, WY–f**

Yankees, VT–y

Zulu, **LA–z**

pilots. *see* people

Places to Visit, **AL–s, AL–z,** GA–a, MS–n, OH–s, WV–z, **WY–v**. *see also* Famous Places

    aquariums, **FL–u,** KY–z, **MD–i,** NE–z, NM–q, OH–z, WA–z

    Butterfly World, FL–z

    city parks, AZ–v

    Corn Palace, **SD–c**

    dude ranches, WY–b

    effigy sites, **WI–e**

    EROS, SD–o

    fountains, **MO–v, SD–f**

    ghost towns, AZ–t

    historic sites, KY–y, SD–h

    historical exhibitions, AL–q, MA–j

    homes, famous, **AL–b**

    La Brea Tar Pits, CA–n

    memorials, DC–d, DC–n, **DC–v,** MA–g, MO–a, NH–b, OK–x, **SD–z,** VA–v

    monuments, CO–f, CO–h, DC–g, DC–n, FL–s, IA–x, ID–a, **ID–c,** IN–l, MD–w, **MO–a,** MT–l, NE–g, NE–i, NM–a, **NM–i,** NM–k, NM–n, OR–f, SC–f, SD–j, **SD–m,** UT–v, VT–q, **WA–t, WY–d**

    mounds, IA–n

    museums, **AL–l, AL–s,** AL–x, **AZ–h,** AZ–m, CO–r, DC–d, DC–p, DC–s, DC–x, DE–d, DE–e, DE–v, DE–w, **DE–z, FL–r, GA–f,** HI–b, IA–j, IN–g, IN–l, IN–q, KS–d, KS–w, **KY–h,** KY–o, **KY–p,** KY–q, KY–r, MA–n, MD–n, MD–r, **MD–v,** MN–h, MN–j, MO–j, MS–c, MT–r, NC–n, ND–h, NE–k, NE–m, NE–o, NE–r, NE–u, NH–e, NH–s, NJ–j, NJ–z, NM–j, NM–q, NM–u, **NY–f,** NY–t, OH–f, OR–m, SC–h, SD–t, TN–e, **VA–w,** VT–g, VT–w, WA–x, WI–m, **WI–q**

    museums, living, CT–u, **MA–v**

    national forests, AK–r, CO–w, ID–f, **KY–n,** NE–a, NM–e, OR–d, WA–e, WV–a, **WY–n**

    national heritage areas, PA–o

    national historic landmarks, CA–w, GA–g, MD–a

    national historic parks, IN–v, NM–a, WA–n

    national historic sites, NC–f, ND–v, OR–m

    national historic trails, NE–g, NE–h

    national landmarks, DE–w, **IA–g,** IA–p, IA–v, IA–x

    national natural landmarks, MD–m

    national parks, AK–d, AZ–g, **AZ–p,** CA–a, CA–r, CA–y, CO–e, **CO–m,** CO–n, HI–v, **MT–g,** ND–n, ND–t, ND–v, **NV–n,** NV–t, OR–i, **SD–b,** SD–j, TX–r, **UT–a, UT–z, WY–g,** WY–o, **WY–y**

    national preserves, KS–u

    national recreation areas, AZ–l, OR–h, **WV–s**

    national scenic areas, **OR–g**

    national scenic trails, **WI–i**

    national wildlife refuges, **DE–r**

    natural attractions, **AK–n, CO–g,** CO–p, **KS–q, KY–n, MO–o, NH–o, NM–i,** OR–l, **TN–l, WI–w** (*see also* Famous Places, waterfalls)

    state forests, WV–k

    state historical parks, CA–x, NE–i, NM–b

    state historical sites, NC–q

    state parks, CT–d, DE–i, **DE–j,** GA–m, ID–d, MD–f, MD–m, **MN–i,** MN–u, **NJ–h, NJ–l,** NV–p, **NY–n,** OH–n, OK–b, **OK–d,** OR–p, OR–v, SD–k, **SD–n,** WA–g, WV–x

    theme parks, NC–x

    World Heritage Sites, AZ–g

    zoos, CO–z, **DC–z, IL–z, KY–z, MD–z, MI–z,** MO–i, **NE–z, OH–z, OR–z, PA–z, TX–z, WA–z, WI–z**

plains. *see* geography

plants, **CO–y,** FL–g, **SC–i**. *see also* agriculture

    berries, **AK–c,** NJ–c, **OR–m**

cactus, AZ–d, **AZ–s, ND–x, TX–p**
carnivorous, **SC–v**
desert, AZ–d, **AZ–s, TX–y**
endangered, **OH–d**
flowers, **AK–f,** AL–u, AR–t, AZ–s, **CA–p,** CO–i, CO–w, **CT–m, DC–r, DE–p, FL–o, GA–c, GA–y, HI–f, HI–l, IA–w, ID–j, IL–v, IN–p, KS–s, KY–g,** MA–m, MD–b, ME–f, **ME–j,** MI–a, **MN–p, MO–d, MS–m, NC–d, ND–w, ND–y, NE–y, NH–l, NJ–v, NM–y, NV–s,** NY–x, OH–c, **OK–m, OR–r, PA–d, RI–v, SC–y, SD–p, TN–d, TX–b, TX–u, UT–s, VA–d, VT–r,** WA–f, WV–f, **WY–i**
fruits, DE–p, FL–o, GA–p, ID–v, MI–c, NY–m, OH–j, RI–a, VT–o, WA–a, WI–c, WV–t
gardens, **AL–b,** CO–v, **DC–k, DE–e, FL–g,** GA–t, **MA–d, NC–m, ND–p, NJ–g, NM–x, OH–h, SC–s,** SC–z, **UT–x**
grass, NV–z
grasses, CO–g, **IL–b,** KS–u, **KY–b**
kudzu, **GA–k**
nuts, **GA–n,** MO–w
rain forests, **HI–r**
trees, AK–r, **AK–s, AR–t, CO–b,** CO–j, **CO–k,** CT–x, **DC–b, DC–t, DE–a, DE–p,** FL–f, **GA–l,** HI–e, **IA–o,** ID–b, **ID–f, IL–w, IN–t, KY–t, MA–e, ME–f,** MI–a, **MI–e, MN–f, MN–r, MO–d, MO–w,** MS–m, MS–u, MT–t, NC–a, **ND–u, NE–a, NE–y, NJ–q,** NM–f, NV–c, **NV–t, OH–b,** OH–j, **OR–d,** PA–d, RI–v, **SC–a, SC–p,** SD–p, **TN–a, TN–d, TX–p, VA–d, VT–m, WA–e,** WA–w, WI–n, WI–s, **WV–t, WY–q**
vegetables, **AK–v, GA–v, IA–k, NC–s, NJ–t,** NM–r
water, **CA–k**
weeds, **MT–k**
wildflowers, FL–c, GA–c, NC–m

politicians. *see* people
politics. *see* government; people
Pony Express. *see* communications, mail service
prairie. *see* geography
puppets, **MS–k**

Q

queens. *see* people, royalty

R

radio. *see* communications; entertainment; inventions
railroads. *see* transportation
rain forests, **AK–r,** AK–s, **HI–r**
ranching. *see* agriculture
recreation, AZ–l, DE–r, FL–l, ME–k, MN–f, **MO–t,** MO–v, **MS–g,** NE–n, NJ–h, VA–s, WA–r, **WI–i**. *see also* sports
  bicycling, IA–r
  hiking, **AR–h**
  kites, **WA–k**
  Rails-to-Trails, OH–x, **PA–r**
  scuba diving, VT–u
  water sports, ID–r
  yachting, **DE–y,** MI–y
reefs, FL–k, FL–q, GA–r
religion, **HI–y**. *see also* people, religious groups
  Native American, AZ–k
reservations, **WA–q**
restaurants, **OK–e**
rivers. *see* geography; transportation
roads. *see* transportation
rocks. *see* geology

Discover America State by State Teacher's Guide

S

sand dunes. *see* geography

satellites. *see* communications; technology

schools, **GA–f, IN–s,** PA–m

    kindergarten, **WI–k**

science, ID–t, NY–l, **OR–x**. *see also* inventions; people, scientists; technology

    astronomy, **AZ–a, HI–h, MN–n, WA–g,** WV–n (*see also* natural phenomena, meteors and meteorites)

    atomic energy, **NM–l**

    atomic research, WA–h

    biology, HI–t

    electricity, **HI–e,** ID–c, KS–z, **NV–h,** NY–n, PA–i, TN–k, WY–u

shells, **FL–h**

ships. *see* industry, ship building; military; transportation, boats; transportation, ships

shipwrecks. *see* transportation, ships

shoes. *see* clothing

singers. *see* people, musicians

slavery, CT–u, KS–f, MO–c, **VA–e,** VA–r, VA–z, VT–c. *see also* people, abolitionists; wars, Civil War

    songs, TN–j

    Underground Railroad, **DE–u, IN–u, MD–t, NE–x,** NY–n, **OH–u, PA–u, RI–u**

soldiers. *see* people, Civil War figures; people, military figures; people, Revolutionary War figures; wars

songs, **AL–n, CO–o, CT–y,** DC–j, **KY–s, MA–j**. *see also* state symbols

    national anthem, **MD–k**

    slave songs, TN–j

    yodeling, **TN–y**

space. *see also* technology

    UFOs, **NM–u**

space program, **AL–x,** AZ–m, **FL–n**

speeches, **PA–g**

sports, MN–f. *see also* people, sports figures; recreation

    automobile racing, **IN–m, NC–z**

    baseball, **AR–z, KY–l, MD–y, ND–h, NJ–u, OK–v, PA–w**

    basketball, **IN–b, KS–b, MA–b**

    equestrian, **KY–e**

    facilities, **LA–s**

    fishing, AL–w, FL–l, **ID–l,** LA–t, MO–r, MT–c, SD–g, **VT–f** (*see also* events)

    football, **AL–f, AR–r, MD–u,** MN–v, **NE–r,** NJ–u, **OK–f, WI–p,** WV–u

    golf, GA–s, WV–w

    hockey, MN–h, NH–z

    horse-racing, **KY–j, KY–r, MD–p**

    hunting (*see* hunting)

    ice climbing, CO–o

    jousting, **MD–j**

    kayaking, CO–k

    Olympics, TN–a, UT–w

    rock climbing, **OK–q,** SD–n, WV–s

    rodeos (*see* events)

    running, IA–b

    skating, roller, NE–r

    skiing, cross-country, **CO–x, VT–x, WI–x**

    skiing, snow, CO–a, **CO–v, ID–k, NH–t, OR–t, UT–q, VT–x,** WV–m

    sled-dog racing, AK–i

    softball, **MN–k**

    water sports, CO–k, HI–o, ID–r, **MS–g,** NJ–n, **RI–y,** SD–g, WV–r

    winter, MI–w, **MN–z,** ND–i, NH–z

state symbols

   amphibians, AL–r, NH–l

   animals, **CA–b, CO–j, CT–s,** FL–d, MO–m, **MT–u, NH–d,** NJ–j, **NV–a, PA–d, SC–l,** WV–b

   animals, aquatic, MO–r

   animals, domesticated, **WI–d**

   animals, marine, **CA–o, DE–h**

   animals, wild, KY–v, **TN–r, WI–w**

   beverages, **OH–t,** OR–m, PA–m, SC–t, **VT–d,** WI–d

   birds, **AK–p, AL–y, AR–m, AZ–w, CA–q, CO–l, CT–a, DE–b, FL–m, GA–b, HI–b, IA–e,** ID–m, **IL–c, IN–c, KS–m,** KY–a, **LA–p, MD–o, MI–r, MN–l, MO–d,** MT–w, NC–d, NC–s, ND–w, **NE–y,** NH–d, **NJ–y,** NM–w, **NV–b,** NY–x, OH–c, **OR–y,** PA–d, **RI–r, SC–w,** SD–p, **TN–m,** TX–m, **UT–g, VT–h, WA–w, WI–r,** WV–b

   birds, game, AL–k

   boats, historical, NC–o

   butterflies, AL–b, CA–g, **DE–t, FL–z, GA–t,** ID–m, **IL–m, KY–v,** OR–y, **SC–e, TN–z, UT–b,** WV–b

   cookies, NM–f

   crustaceans, **MD–b**

   dances, **CO–s,** MO–f, ND–d

   dishes, **TX–c**

   dogs, MD–c, **NC–p,** PA–d, VA–d, **WI–a**

   fish, **AK–k,** AL–j, CA–g, **FL–q,** ID–l, IL–b, KY–v, **MA–c,** MI–b, **MN–w,** MO–r, MT–c, ND–n, NE–y, OR–c, PA–d, RI–v, WA–f, **WI–m,** WV–b

   fish, cold-water, VT–f

   fish, freshwater, FL–l

   fish, saltwater, FL–d

   fish, warm-water, VT–f

   flags, **AK–f,** AL–m, **AR–f,** AZ–c, **CA–b,** CO–c, **CT–f, DE–f, FL–f,** HI–k, IA–s, ID–e, **IN–f, KS–s, KY–u, MA–f,** MD–b, MD–o, **MO–g,** MT–t, NC–t, **ND–e,** NJ–j, **NM–z, NV–f, NY–x, OR–u, PA–y,** RI–o, **SC–p, TN–f,** TX–i, **WA–f, WI–y, WV–f**

   flagships, **PA–s**

   flowers, **AK–f,** AR–t, AZ–s, **CA–p,** CO–w, **CT–m, DE–p, FL–o, GA–c, HI–f, IA–w, ID–j, IL–v, IN–p, KS–s, KY–g,** KY–u, MA–m, MD–b, ME–f, **MI–a, MN–p, MO–d, MS–m,** MT–b, **NC–d, ND–w, NE–y, NH–l, NJ–v,** NM–y, **NV–s,** NY–x, OH–c, PA–d, **RI–v, SC–y, TX–b, UT–s, VA–d, VT–r,** WA–f, **WI–v,** WV–f, **WY–i**

   fossils, CO–f, CT–d, **DE–h,** ID–a, IL–t, KY–v, **MS–z,** MT–d, ND–l, NE–i, NV–i, **SD–t,** UT–u, WA–c

   fruits, **DE–p, FL–o, ID–v,** NJ–c, **RI–a,** TX–v, **VT–o,** WV–t

   gems, AK–j, CO–a, FL–n, **GA–q, HI–g,** ID–g, ME–r, **MN–a,** MT–t, **NV–o, NY–g,** OR–s, **TN–u, TX–g, UT–t, VT–g,** WA–g

   grain, **MN–w, WI–y**

   grasses, CO–g, NV–z

   horses, ID–a, ND–n

   insects, AK–f, AL–b, **AR–i, CO–i, CT–p,** DE–t, **GA–h,** ID–m, IL–m, **MO–h, NC–h,** NE–f, **NE–y,** NJ–g, **NM–w,** NY–l, **OH–l,** OR–y, PA–d, SD–p, **TN–h,** TN–z, **TX–m, UT–b,** VA–i, **WA–d,** WV–b

   instruments, **MO–f**

   mammals, **AZ–r, MI–w,** NC–a, NE–y, OH–n, TX–m, UT–e

   mammals, marine, FL–u, **GA–r**

   mammals, saltwater, **FL–d**

   mammals, small, **TX–n**

   mammals, water, **MS–b**

   mascots, AL–b

minerals, AK–x, **AR–q**, CA–g, NV–f, RI–v, **WI–g**

mottos, IA–s, ID–e, **IN–x**, **KY–u**, MA–f, **MN–n**, MT–t, **NY–x**, OR–u, PA–y, RI–i, **TX–f**, UT–b, WV–f

muffins, NY–m

neckwear, **AZ–b**

nicknames, **AR–n**, **CA–g**, **CO–c**, CT–h, **CT–n**, IA–h, **ID–g**, IN–h, KY–b, **ME–d**, ME–f, **MN–g**, **MO–s**, **MT–b**, **MT–t**, NC–t, ND–g, **NE–c**, **NM–e**, OH–b, OR–b, **PA–k**, RI–o, SD–p, TN–v, VA–o, WA–e, **WI–b**, WV–m

nuts, MO–w, OR–n

peppers, **TX–j**

plants, **MA–c**, TX–p

prairie grasses, **IL–b**

precious stone, NC–a

questions, NM–r

quilts, **AL–q**

reptiles, **AL–r**, **AZ–r**, **FL–a**, **LA–a**, **MI–p**, **NC–e**, **NV–r**

rivers, NE–d

rocks, **IA–g**, **MA–r**, MO–l, NC–a, **OR–e**, RI–v, **VT–g**

salutes, NM–z

seals, **AL–a**, **AR–g**, AZ–c, **DE–x**, FL–f, **IA–s**, **ID–e**, KY–u, LA–p, MO–g, **NJ–j**, **NV–g**, **OR–u**, **VT–s**, WV–f

shellfish, CT–o

shells, AL–j, NC–o, **NJ–k**, **TX–l**

soft drinks, NE–k

songs, **CO–w**, CT–y, **HI–s**, **KY–s**, NV–s, OK–h, **WI–o**

sports, AK–i, **MD–j**

stones, IN–w, MI–p

trees, **AK–s**, AL–b, AR–t, **CA–r**, **CO–b**, CT–x, **DE–a**, **DE–p**, FL–f, **GA–l**, HI–e, **IA–o**, ID–f, **IL–w**, **IN–t**, **KY–t**, **MA–e**, **ME–f**, **MI–e**, **MN–r**, **MO–d**, MS–m, MT–t, NC–a, **ND–u**, NE–a, **NE–y**, NJ–q, NM–f, **NV–t**, **OH–b**, **OR–d**, PA–d, **RI–v**, **SC–p**, SD–p, **TN–a**, **TX–p**, **VA–d**, **VT–m**, WA–w, WI–s, WV–t, **WY–q**

vegetables, GA–v, NM–r

waterfowl, **MS–w**

wildflowers, FL–c, GA–c

statehood, AR–f, CO–c, **DE–f**, DE–p, IA–d, **IN–j**, KS–t, ME–a, **MN–h**, MO–g, **ND–c**, NJ–j, NM–s, OH–o, **OK–n**, VT–c

statehouse. *see* Famous Places, capitols

sunlight, continuous, AK–v

swamps. *see* geography

symbols of Washington D.C.

    trees, DC–t

    bird, **DC–w**

symbols, national. *see* national symbols

symbols, state. *see* state symbols

technology, IA–u, **ID–t**, UT–i. *see also* inventions; science

    computers, WA–m

    dams, **AL–w**, **NV–h**

    locks and dams, **AL–w**

    National Radio Astronomy Observatory, WV–n

    satellite observation, **SD–o**

    space travel, **AL–x**, **FL–n**, TX–h

    television, **ID–t**

    windmills, HI–e, KS–z, **MA–x**, **NE–w**, **TX–w**

telegraph. *see* communications; inventions

telephone. *see* communications

television. *see* communications; entertainment; industry, entertainment; inventions

terrorism, **NY–w, OK–x,** VA–p

tides, **ME–t**

time zones. *see* geography

tornadoes. *see* weather

tourism. *see* industry

toys. *see* games and toys

traditions, **DC–e, DC–t, LA–k,** MD–p

   Hispanic, **ID–q**

   Native American, NM–d

Trail of Tears, GA–c, **OK–t, TN–t**

trails. *see* recreation; transportation, roads and trails

trains. *see* transportation, railroads

transportation, **NM–t**

   airplanes, AK–j, **AR–x, DC–x, KS–a, NC–k,** NJ–f, WA–b

   automobiles, **IN–k,** MI–d, **MI–q**

   bicycles, CO–s

   boats, AK–a, AK–j, **AK–u,** AK–y, AL–w, DE–n, **DE–y,** GA–s, **HI–h,** HI–p, **IL–r, MD–s, ME–o,** MI–y, MO–r, **MS–q,** ND–o, ND–u, **NH–g,** OH–m, RI–y, SC–g (*see also* transportation, ships; transportation, submarines)

   bridges, **AL–k, CO–**r, **FL–k, MA–u, MI–b,** MN–d, MO–a, **NC–g, NE–m, NH–x, NY–b, OH–y,** OR–a, VA–t, **VT–b**

   canals, **DE–c, IL–i, NY–e**

   coaches, **NH–c**

   cog railways, CO–o, NH–t

   dogsleds, AK–i

   handcarts, NE–j, **UT–h**

   hot air balloons, **MS–h, NM–h**

   locks and dams, **AL–w**

   oxcarts, **ND–o**

   railroads, **DC–u,** ID–g, **ID–u, IL–n, IL–x,** IN–o, **KS–a,** KS–d, KS–h, **MD–r,** MO–a, MO–v, **MT–x,** NC–q, **NC–x,** ND–c, **NE–u,** NJ–f, NM–t, NV–g, NY–e, PA–o, PA–r, TX–c, **UT–r,** VA–v, WV–g, **WV–x, WY–k**

   rivers, AK–y, AL–w, CT–q, DC–p, **IA–r,** IN–e, **IN–o,** KY–o, MS–r, MT–y, NE–e, NH–g, OH–m, OR–g, WV–g, WV–r

   roads and trails, AK–i, CA–m, CO–t, CO–w, DE–c, **ID–o,** IN–x, KS–d, KS–i, KY–d, **KY–w,** MA–e, ME–k, MO–t, **MS–n,** NC–y, **NE–h, NE–j, NH–k,** NJ–h, NM–s, NM–t, **OK–d,** OR–g, **OR–o, TX–c, TX–e,** VA–s, **WY–x**

   rockets, **AL–x**

   sheepwagons, **WY–s**

   ships, AL–u, **DE–k, DE–z, MA–m, MD–d, ME–w, ME–x,** MI–x, MN–d, NJ–f, NJ–n, **OH–s, RI–g, VT–u** (*see also* transportation, boats)

   submarines, **SC–x**

   tramways, NM–t

   trucks, NJ–f

   tunnels, VA–t

   wagons, covered, NC–y, NE–j

trees. *see* plants; state symbols

tsunamis. *see* disasters, natural

U

universities. *see* colleges and universities

V

valleys. *see* geography

veterans. *see* wars

village green, **NH–v**

volcanoes. *see* geology

W

War for Independence. *see* wars, Revolutionary War

wars, **MD–f, ME–e,** TN–v. *see also* military; people, military figures

   American Red Cross, DC–a

   battles, **MT–l**

   Civil War, AL–d, AL–u, **AL–y,** DC–a, DC–b, DC–d, DC–f, **IL–l,** KS–f, **KY–y, MD–h, MO–c,** MS–l, **MS–v,** NC–t, NV–f, **PA–g, SC–j,** WV–f, WV–h, WV–j (*see also* people, Civil War figures)

   memorials to, **DC–v**

   Revolutionary War, CT–k, DE–b, IN–v, **MA–b, MA–l, MA–o,** NJ–t, NJ–w, NJ–x, NY–t, **PA–v, SC–f, VA–y** (*see also* people, Revolutionary War figures)

   submarines, **SC–x**

   War of 1812, LA–j, OH–e, PA–s

   World War I, DC–w

   World War II, ID–p, **KS–i, NE–v, OK–u, SD–u**

water, AZ–z, ID–i, **MO–b, UT–i**. *see also* geography; transportation

   dams, MS–g, **NV–h**

   irrigation, **WA–y**

   reservoirs, **MA–q**

   tidal pools, DC–c

   tsunamis, **HI–t**

   xeriscaping, **NM–x, UT–x**

weather, CA–d, **HI–w, LA–u,** MA–y, **MN–z, ND–i,** NE–t, **NH–z,** PA–p, **VT–k**

   Dust Bowl, **OK–d**

   hurricanes, **LA–h**

   tornadoes, **KS–t, OK–c, OK–w**

   wind, **KS–z, RI–z**

women. *see* government, women's rights; people

Writer's Workshop, IA–u

Notes

Notes

Notes

Notes